FAIRGROUND HERITAGE

VOLUME ONE

AN AGE OF ACHIEVEMENT

PETER WILKES

When the Fair invaded the peace of Oxford... ***(Author's Collection)***

FOREWORD

by Ray Tunnicliff, Chairman of the Fairground Society

When I was first given a copy of this book to read and asked to write a foreword for it, I felt somewhat surprised. Having read, 'An Age of Achievement', the first in a series of three books by Peter Wilkes covering the story of 'Our Fairground Heritage', I can only say that I feel very happy to be able to do this.

The book has been carefully written to give both the layman as well as the hardened enthusiast an insight into the development and role in society of the fairground and the people who have travelled with the fairs. As well as being historically correct it is beautifully laced with personal anecdotes of the showmen which makes it so interesting.

The author has worked for many years as a reporter for the 'World's Fair', the showman's newspaper, and this book reveals that not only has he been a good reporter, but he has obviously become a friend to many of the fairground fraternity.

The photographs used to illustrate the book are first class, many being supplied by the showmen theirselves. I am sure that all who read the book will enjoy it as I did, and the showmen will accept it as a window through which the layman can see the development of the travelling fair. Now read on.

INTRODUCTION

To the casual visitor, fairs are cloaked in mystery. True they have a magic that no other form of entertainment can equal, but the show people are in cities, towns and villages for only a short time each year. Thus, without understanding, there is a tendency for this hard working class of society to be dismissed as mere itinerant travellers.

Fairs are fighting a constant battle for survival. A move from a traditional site to some backwater can spell disaster for a way of life that is part of our great heritage. And yet the uninitiated continue in many parts of the country to demand the removal of fairs.

This was partly the reason for this book, to state a case for both the show people and the travelling fair. But even among enthusiasts for whom the fair presents genuine pleasure, and who look upon the show people as friends, there is possibly a tendency to forget its beginnings and concentrate instead on its immediate past and present.

Here was the second reason for this particular volume. To show that through hard work and endeavour those early showmen and their successors brought about 'an age of achievement' that equals almost anything recorded in the commercial world, and in fact betters many industrial records.

CHAPTER ONE

FAIRS AND THEIR ORIGINS

Fairs have a long and noteworthy history, and some so long that they cannot even trace their first beginnings. For in those remote times, when most communities obtained a large degree of self sufficiency and travel was both difficult and dangerous, specialised merchants came to the buyers at fairs throughout the country and goods could be purchased to cover the needs until the next fair, possibly a year later.

These merchant fairs originated in many ways, some were centred on the great medieval religious houses, usually held on the feast day of the saint to whom the abbey, priory or other religious house was dedicated. Thus originated the only fair held within the City of London, Bartholomew Fair. Raphere, Henry I's minstrel founded the priory, hospital and church of St Bartholomew in 1102 and secured the grant of a three day cloth fair from the King as income to the priory. Held in the Great Smithfield, it was the greatest of all the summer fairs and became renowned as a cloth market all over the world.

Fairs could only be started by Royal Charter or Act of Parliament. However, those fairs whose charter cannot today be traced are deemed to be fairs by ancient prescription or originally to have been subject to a royal grant.

A typical country fair of religious origin was Stowe Green, a fair established in 1268, when King Henry III granted a 'yearly fair at the Manor of Stowe, in the County of Lincoln, on the vigil, the feast and the morrow of St John the Baptist' to the Prior and convent of Sempringham Priory. This was one of the most important monasteries in the county and the head of the Gilbertine Order, which in its prime had sixty canons and two hundred nuns. Country folk came to buy their goods from booths and stalls set up in a field at the side of crossroads, close to the old medieval Brigend Causeway. This linked the rich fenlands with the uplands to the west. Its proximity to two other major roads made it accessible to goods from further away, an ideal site for a trading fair.

Such fairs were prime assets to the likes of Sempringham Priory, for they brought in tolls to the Prior. Pleasure, equally with business, must, however, have entered into them from early times, as the word 'fair' itself comes partly from the Latin 'feriae' for holidays, as well as from 'forum' or market place.

Stourbridge Fair, near Cambridge, was another of the great fairs of the Middle Ages, granted by King John to a nearby Leper Hospital.

Romantics, however, would have us believe otherwise, for they say that the fair resulted from a company of Westmorland cloth dealers being overtaken by a storm on the outskirts of Cambridge, and nearly losing their goods in the waters of the Cam and Stour. Those Kendal clothiers, so we are told, fished out their bales and spread their goods to dry on Stourbridge Common. So many townsfolk came to see and buy that all the stock was speedily sold, and the clothiers returned to Kendal without having visited Norwich, their intended destination. They are said to have returned the following year and were joined by other traders in such numbers that the booths were arranged in orderly streets: Garlic Row, Booksellers' Row, Cook Row and many more. In the Draper's section, called the 'Duddery', it is reputed that over 100,000 worth of woollens were sold in a single week. While the town of Cambridge claimed certain rights, it was the University that had the rights of proclaiming the fair and it was to its officers that the duties fell of testing all weights and measures used at it, and of viewing all goods, and of regulating and where necessary, punishing persons offending against the laws.

The laws regulating prices and quality were very strict

and the proclamation or 'crying the fair' was a lengthy business. There was a daily court of justice, the 'Court of Pie Powder', a name with Norman-French origins, as a court of 'Pieds Pourdreux', or 'Court of Dusty Feet', an allusion to the itinerant character of most of the fair users.

At such great commercial gatherings as these, not all the goods would be value for money. In the fifteenth century the manufacturers and merchants of London and other large towns sent representatives to the fairs to examine and seize any faulty merchandise. This was often a pretext of merchants in the city who were jealous of the business done at places like Stourbridge and they tried from time to time to restrict trading. One of their excuses was that any leftovers when the fairs finished were sold throughout the country at knock down prices because the profits had already been made at the fairs, and this hurt local merchants.

Our heritage fairs, however, were not only meeting places for English merchants. Many, like the Boston fair, brought together merchants from the Low Countries, Italy, Norway, Germany, the Baltic ports, France, Spain and Gascony. Now a May fair, it has rightly been described as 'modern magic with roots in the past'. For here is a part of Lincolnshire history that dates back to the thirteenth century, to the days when peace was being made between England and Wales at Worcester. Such was its importance that it was held over an eight day period and was opened by the Sheriff of Lincoln. Customers at this great annual gathering included representatives of the royal household, who travelled to the port to buy silks and satins and the Canons of Bridlington who attended regularly from 1290 to 1335 to purchase 'groceries and cloth' for the convent. The merchandise traded at the fair covered almost every conceivable commodity, cattle and sheep, corn and fodder, cloth, wool and leather, wine and lace, these and many other goods changed hands at Boston.

Problems, however, were not unknown. Edward III sent a jury to the town to enquire into an allegation that the 'lords of the fair of St Botolph let the dealing continue beyond the dates set by the charter'. They faced an acute dilemma. If they found for the king they would incur the displeasure of that Lord of the Fair, the Earl of Richmond. To find for him would have displeased the king. It was a case for compromise and they reported that not knowing the exact dates of the charter they were unable to say if they had been exceeded or not.

Boston owed its prominence to its port, then the second largest in the country. Trade was particularly good with the Low Countries and the Hanseatic League, and for the fair some fifteen German ships could be expected yearly.

The town, however, favoured its own merchants when it came to trade. The Mayor's permission had to be obtained by outside merchants and this involved a heavy payment. To work without this permission not only resulted in imprisonment, but the confiscation of stock. One Stamford trader found himself behind bars and without his stock of 7,000 pins and leather gloves for breaking that regulation.

The Mayor and the Town Magistrates must have found the fair a busy period. They had to continually patrol it to uphold the law. On occasions their journeys would take them round both main and back streets of the town. For in 1575 an order was given for the residents to ease the passage of strangers in the dark by hanging a lighted lantern outside their homes between 6pm and 9pm. Those who ignored the order would find themselves paying over a one shilling penalty for each occasion their oil lamp was out.

Another form of fair came into being after the Black Death, for the acute shortage of labour that resulted from this 14th century plague brought about the Statute of Labourers. This required all able bodied men to present themselves annually for hiring at a stated wage. These hiring fairs were usually held around Michaelmas, the end of the farming year.

In the Midlands they were known as 'Mop Fairs', a name derived from the way those waiting for hire indicated their trade by an emblem or token. The shepherd wore a tuft of wool, the carters had a piece of plated whipcord in their hats and the thatcher strands of straw. Girls were also there, offering their services as domestics. They waited while farmers came and bargained with them. When an agreement was struck up, the men proceeded to fix coloured ribbons in their hats and did their best to have a merry time with the retainer paid. The rustics used to patronise a tailor's stall, bespeake a suit of clothes, wear it for a year and pay for it at the next fair.

The Hiring fairs were a vital part of rural life and in Loughborough men and girls stood about in groups, often with a wooden box or tin trunk containing the worker's worldly possessions ready to be transported to a new home. Contracts were by word of mouth, but very rarely broken. However, there were problems relating to the Poor Law position. Employment was usually for a day short of year, and to qualify for Poor Law treatment, there had to be regular residence in the parish for a year and parishes tried to avoid their Poor Rate being burdened by newcomers.

In 1866, Corby Glen's May Statute Hiring Fair was described in a Lincolnshire writing as 'A very large one and with more hirers than servants'. However, eleven years later there was a note that 'Corby statutes very poor, scarcely anyone here'. Two years later they were 'very poor indeed'.

The First World War and the decline in the agricultural work force in the more mechanised post war period brought the practice of hiring labour at the statute fairs almost to an end. Before the war, however, the Grantham May Fair had become one of the most important days in the local calendar. This larger event had overtaken the smaller village hiring fairs after the arrival of the railways, which came to Corby Glen in 1852.

On the Saturday of May week, the men would stand in the Market Place, each trade in a line and with symbols in their buttonholes. The farmers would pass by and examine the prospective employees. On being hired a man would be given a shilling as a 'fastening token'.

Not only was the statute fair the occasion for changing jobs, it was an outing for the families when new sets of clothes were bought. Such was the importance of Grantham Statute Fair to country dwellers that the year before the war, on 24th May, 1913, 420 cheap tickets were issued by the Great Northern Railway from Corby, now the rail centre for that area, to Grantham.

There were also horse fairs at places such as Barnet, livestock fairs as at Chesterfield, cheese fairs, and often villages as small as Corby Glen would hold a sheep fair. This was separate from the hiring fairs, and has survived through to modern times, although the entertainment side has all but disappeared.

Corby Glen is a graphic example of the decline, of not only the small country fair, but village and agricultural life itself. Yet in the beginning, by a charter granted in 1238, Corby Glen was entitled to not one fair but three. And in addition there were rights to hold a market each Thursday. Two of the fairs were hiring fairs and the third, the Autumn event, was the sheep fair that exists today. The fortunes of this fair, held on the first Monday before October 10th, reflect the conditions of the village and its farming community over the past two centuries. There is little doubt that the financial farming year was centred on the fair. At fair time farmers would sell their cattle and horses as well as sheep to both settle outstanding accounts and bring in the income for the immediate future. Although, by the end of the eighteenth century the fair, like local agriculture, was in decline, the following century saw an upsurge in its fortunes. Indeed, in 1863 a record was made of 'the largest show of sheep, cattle and horses that has ever been seen on the ground'. There was even talk of making it a two day event, something that must have seemed even more feasible the following year when ninety three truck loads of livestock left by train alone. Nor was it confined to livestock. As sheep and cattle dominated the village green, the Market Place was filled with amusements of every kind. Swing boats and roundabouts, shooting galleries and boxing booths, not forgetting the market traders who brought their stalls to the village, added to the Corby attraction for people from surrounding villages.

Fair week, particularly the Monday when the cattle trading took place, was a true 'red letter' period in the village's annual calendar. The cattle drovers, the buyers and other sellers, all lodged at local hostelries if they had travelled far. It was a time for family get togethers, reunions that were were made easy following the arrival of the Great Northern Railway. The womenfolk would be committed to the kitchen baking the cakes and pies that were needed to satisfy visiting appetites in a menu that was topped by that Lincolnshire delicacy, stuffed chine. 1876, however, showed its peak with some 12,000 sheep offered for sale. The agricultural depression of the last quarter of the nineteenth century hit Corby hard. At its end that had halved and in the year before the First World War there was but a third of that number of sheep penned and a few other animals. By the time the 1930s arrived, horse and cattle dealing was finished and with the decline in livestock sales, the amusement and other trading activities declined.

The arrival of the internal combustion engine, the closure of the railway station in 1959 all continued Corby's decline. And while the sheep fair continues to this day, the amusement side is a part of the past. Attempts are being made to rekindle interest in the pleasure side, but the days when the Market Place was a mecca for pleasure seekers of all kinds can never return in the days when sheep arrive by road early on the Monday morning and have all departed the village that same day.

1. St. Bartholomew's Fair in the 18th century with Richardson's Theatre Booth and a roundabout on the left with sedan chairs to ride in. In 1708 this fourteen day fair was reduced to three, although in 1739 an extra day was added. However, in 1843 the Corporation banned the Mart. ***(Author)***

2. Chesterfield Market Place in 1882. Just over one hundred years ago the September cattle fair was being held in what was then and is now, the town's normal market area. *(Chesterfield Markets Department)*

3. An eighteenth century engraving of a Cheese Fair. *(Author)*

4. Life on the fair ground where a family are seen doing their washing at the Barnet fair. *(Author)*

5. The opening of Chipping Norton Mop Fair in 1933 by the Mayor, Alderman W.C. Hannis. *(Author)*

6. A traditional scene at Mitchem where the key was symbolic of the opening of a fair through a Charter that was said to have been granted by Queen Elizabeth 1st after a petition by Sir Walter Raleigh. *(Author)*

7. Fairgoers in Broad Street, Stamford, circa 1905. *(Author)*

8. Crowds flock to Lincoln Fair in 1907. ***(Author)***

9. The fairground scene in the early 1930s. This was at Chesterfield and is believed to be on the racecourse. ***(Author)***

10. An undated photograph of the opening at King's Lynn. Note the religious banner on the left of the photograph. ***(Roger Tuby)***

11. A 1907 photograph of Gloucester fair with Symond's rides and horse drawn living vans. *(Author)*

12. The 1920s scene with children passing through an unnamed fair. *(Author)*

CHAPTER TWO

CANDY FLOSS AND MUSHY PEAS

Some fairs adopted and retained the name associated with their trading commodity. One of the most famous examples is Nottingham's historic Goose Fair, whose origins go back to a charter granted by King Edward I in 1284. This was for an eight day September fair, held at the Feast of St Matthew. However, it was almost three centuries later, in 1541, that the name 'Goose Fair' was entered in the borough records, when the Chamberlain's accounts itemised 22d for the stalls which the Sheriffs had on Goose Fair Day. The name was derived from the geese, raised on the stubble fields of Lincolnshire and Norfolk, which were at their peak in time for what was then a Michaelmas fair. More than 20,000 protesting geese would find their way to Nottingham into eager buying hands for what was the traditional Michaelmas meal.

In those days of primitive transport and equally primitive roads, there was no alternative for the drovers but to walk. Before starting out the bird's feet were dipped into a protective mixture of tar and sand. There was no mention, however, of the feet of the men who had to control these flocks of hungry geese for hundreds of miles.

Yet not everyone agrees that it was birds of the feathered variety that brought the fair its name. Romantics recall a certain Squire whose experiences with the fair sex had been such that he determined his only son, who had been motherless since infancy, should only be aware of ladies when he was of that 'age of discretion'. Then our Squire had the fatal idea of introducing his son to the fair. Not only was the fair a new experience for him but he was seeing Nottingham's pretty girls for the first time. 'What are they father?' he asked, 'Geese boy, only geese' was the reply. Then, when it was time to leave, the father asked his son what he would like to take home as a fairing. 'A Goose' was the spontaneous answer, 'A goose please'.

Those days of commerce were certainly not without their moments of excitement, as fair goers discovered in 1766, when cheese, a staple food at the time, increased in price by one third. The crowds, enraged at the thoughts of having to pay nearly 4d per pound, began to remonstrate. When words failed it was time for action. Stalls were ransacked and farmers attacked. Within minutes huge cheeses were bowling down the sloping streets, pursuing owners now only concerned with escape. At the height of the trouble the mayor decided to take a hand, positioning himself at a crossroads, arms outstretched, urging the mob to disperse. Alas there was an indignant end when he was flattened by one hundredweight of prime dairy produce! A detachment of Dragoons was called in and peace was restored only after a man had been killed and several others injured. But in the confusion, many families ensured that their larders were well stocked and there is little doubt that living standards were high for some time after the Cheese Riots.

The trading aspects of the fair continued to be important, but in 1813, there was the first hint of future change, with the magistrates banning 'those dangerous and disgraceful machines called merry go rounds'. There was no ban, however, on sideshows. The public, starved of cheap entertainment, responded in style when Wombwell's Wild Beast Show made its appearance in 1805, and for the next 100 years it was to reign supreme. The author William Howitt gave a graphic account of the fair's changing face, 'cages of wild beasts, theatricals, giants, dwarfs and other prodigies and wonders, all manner of wild and peculiar looking people, strollers, beggars, gypsies, dancers, players of harps, Punch and Judy shows and similar artistes.'

The importance of Goose Fair to the entertainment fraternity was shown in both 1819 and 1829, when Madame Tussaud brought her life size wax figures to the city. A room was made available in the Old Exchange, ironically the building whose replacement in 1927-8 lead to the Goose Fair losing its traditional city centre site. The collection was on view daily for twelve hours at an admission price of 1/-, when the normal side show charged 1d. But this was more than a mere waxworks exhibition.

Marie Grosholtz, who was to become Madam Tussaud, learned her wax modelling skills from Dr Philippe Curtius, who set up the first Chamber of Horrors or 'Caverne des grands voleurs', in France and who saw her become proficient in 'death mask' modelling. In 1794 Phillipe Curtius died and Madam Tussaud inherited his waxworks and in 1802 brought them over to England. She realised that ordinary French criminals would be of no interest to a British public, and her Chamber of Horrors, always in a room away from the general waxworks, were from death masks from the revolution era. Those selected to make their English debuts were the assassinated Marat, the infamous newspaper editor, Hebert, Robespierre, Carrier, responsible for mass drownings, and the former Public Prosecutor, Fouquier-Tinville.

It was these 'death mask' waxworks and accompanying historic relics that gave her show a unique flavour. However, her exhibition was always presented with all possible splendour, to educate as well as entertain, and while the public demanded that macabre section, these waxworks were never allowed to sink into sensationalism. In 1808, after periods in Scotland and Ireland, Madam Tussaud announced that she was returning to London. However, it was another twenty seven years before the exhibition settled down in a permanent home in the capital and that time was spent on a marathon tour of the country.

Her visit to Nottingham in 1819 was part of an itinerary that began at Norwich, visiting King's Lynn, Boston, Lincoln and Newark, before finishing at the Goose Fair. More than a mere waxworks exhibitor, she was becoming renowned as a 'travelling journalist'. News at the time circulated by word of mouth, and where there were local newspapers, invariably there were few illustrations. This exhibition, being constantly updated with wax impressions of those in the news, famous people including the Prince Regent and those not so famous, such as Dr. Soloman whose patent medicines were household words, guaranteed to attract the audiences.

Not everyone was welcome at Nottingham, however, and the magistrates again intervened in 1852. The bearded lady in their eyes was definitely unnatural and they decided that the city would be better off without her charms.

The variety at the Goose Fair and, indeed, the other fairs by 1853, must have seemed unbelievable to Victorians, devoid of almost any other pleasures in their lives. Holloway's theatre vended the 'legitimate drama'. He was opposed by Rayners Theatrical Company and Rye's. There was Wombwell's Menagerie which always entered the town preceded by an open wagon from which his excellent brass band entertained onlookers. Wombwell's son-in-law, Mr Edmonds, was there with his highly respectable exhibition of living wonders, and his no less respectable band, which, with the music of the Imperial Mechanical Exhibition close by, presented an enjoyable experience. Winrow's ingenious views, a small portrait painting gallery, a camera obscura and Clapton's views of the Great Exhibition were the mainstays of the Market Place.

There was also the Royal Caledonian Wax Works from St Andrews with their own bagpipers, and the bazaars offered all manner of hard and soft goods, from tripe and oysters to fiddles and lace. The stalls became a mountainous region of toffee and gingerbread, nuts and brandy snaps, there was an array of shooting galleries, and an innumerable variety of scientific machines at which the customers might test their weight, height and strength.

Then two years later the machine age dawned with the appearance of Twigdon's Riding Machine. Primitive it may have been with a circular platform suspended by rods from a centre pole and with a series of horses mounted on the platform, but it was a public fascination. Motive power had to be either by a man in the centre pushing it round or by small boys. Their enticement was the offer of free rides at the end of their stint at machine powering.

And by the 1860s, did we have the first 'pik-a-straw'. For a contemporary writer refers to the men who bought a large quantity of envelopes, inserted paper inside them and told their incredulous audiences that these contained a wonderful secret, so wonderful that they were forbidden to sell them.They were there with large bundles of straws under their arms and the punters paid their half pennies and selected a straw, to win or otherwise, one of these 'secret envelopes'.

While the side shows reigned supreme with only the intrusion of primitive hand operated rides, the 1870s saw a drastic change in fortune. Such was the challenge that mechanical rides began to make against this long held entertainment monopoly, the Market Traders Association demanded a curtailment of the fair and a 'return to semi sanity'.

The trading element left at the fair had a rather unexpected victory in 1876 when, faced by increasing opposition from a sector of the public, the Markets and Fairs Committee's application to the Secretary of State that the previous eight day fair be held on the first Tuesday in October until the following Saturday night was approved. Opposition, however, was not killed off. Two years later an enquiry into the moral, social, sanitary and commercial effects started. Conflicting evidence was given to the enquiry. One employer complained that it was a nuisance, girls would not work and men used it as an excuse for drink. In contrast another business figure felt it a 'necessary relief from the daily cares and toils and the foul atmosphere of factory life'.

Then the Nottingham Town and Country Social Guild reported on alleged disadvantages to trade, health, temperance and morals. Their suggestion that this historic fair be cut to one day, however, went too far, even for the council. By 1880 the abolitionists had secured another victory. That year saw the fair open on the first Thursday in October and continue until the Saturday night, the period it enjoys in the city today.

Restrictions may have been imposed, but the abolitionists who hoped for further cuts failed to take into account its financial appeal to the corporation. In 1883, the income was £594 14s 2d and the following year had increased to more than £636 0s 0d. Further protests were destined to fall on deaf ears. This, however, was a different fairground. The steam revolution brought the railways and reduced the trading aspects of fairs almost overnight. Shops now served local needs and there was no longer a need for buyers and sellers to cover large distances to come together. And as that side slipped towards oblivion, steam, through the work of men like Frederick Savage, transformed the entertainment aspect, releasing showmen from muscle and pony power, bringing undreamed of thrills to an amazed public.

The fair in 1899 featured Bostock and Wombwell's No 1 Menagerie, Professor Burnett's Grand Military Entertainment, Kemp's Famous Prodigies, Walls Royal Life Size Projectorgraph, Terry's Performing Croc, William's Art Exhibition, Lawrence's Marionettes, Sedgewick's No 2 Menagerie, Wallace the celebrated lion, Norman's Human Bear and Animated Pictures, Amye's Working Models, Bosco the Illusionist, Wadbrookes Royal Electrograph and the Bioscopes of Randall Williams and Captain Payne.

The rides included Collin's Mountain Ponies, Venetian Gondolas, Roundabouts and Pneumatic Cycles, a ride from John Collins, Twigdon's Roundabout and Green's Roundabout. Then there were the various side shows and children's attractions and sellers of everything from Nottingham Lace to Grantham Gingerbread.

Progress, however, was destined to overtake the Goose Fair when it lost its city centre site in 1927, with the present Council House rising on the site of the old Exchange Building.

Here, on that final fair on Slab Square on October, 6th, 7th and 8th, the showmen entertained the Nottingham Public in style. Pat Collins brought his Scenic Whales, Scenic Dragons, Spinner and Over The Falls. John Collins took his 48 foot diameter revolving platform horses, and his Steam Yachts. J. Proctor had his Scenic Peacocks, Helter Skelter and Cake Walk. Frederick Cox had his Dolphin Switchback, B. Holland was another with a Cake Walk and the Ashley brothers had revolving platform horses. Arthur Holland had his Scenic Whales and local show woman, Mrs T. Mellor had her Cake Walk. Mrs F. Mellor had revolving platform horses and M Curzon took along two juvenile motor cycles.

This, of course, was in the days of steam and 18 engines are listed in the records. Pat Collins had 5, John Collins 1, J. Proctor 3, Frederick Cox needed two for his Dolphins and there was an engine with each of the two other Cake Walks, The Ashley brothers needed one engine as did Mrs F. Mellors, while Arthur Holland's Scenic Whales had the services of two. The remaining engine was with the Menagerie of E. H. Bostock.

The fair was also made up of 279 other attractions including juveniles, round and side stalls as well as traders and ice cream sellers.

This last fair on the old site brought in £3,026 0s 2d for the council, a figure very similar to the £3,556 8s 10d income from the first fair on the new Forest site. This year saw Pat Collins with eight rides, The Scenic Dragons and Whales, Horses, Helter Skelter, Radio Cars, Hit The Deck, Swish and Over The Falls. John Collins kept his same two rides, but John Proctor had Dragons as well as a circus, the Ashley Brothers added a Cake Walk and a newcomer was James Manders with his Steam Yachts. Wilfred Turner presented a Razzle Dazzle, Enoch Farrar a Devil's Disc, Mike Jarvis the Tunnel Railway and Harry Hall his Scenic Whales. There was, of course, also Wombwell's Menagerie.

The shows included illusions, a Haunted House, distorting mirrors, native dancers, a variety show, rare animals, a midget, two Boxing Booths, working models, a contrast show, a Wild West show, reptiles, lions, water birds and a cyclops. There were 49 large games, 9 juveniles and 53 darts and small games.

This was truly the age of steam on the fairground with that first Forest fair echoing to the sound and smells of 31 Showman's steam traction engines.

13. Bostock and Wombwell's Menagerie at Goose Fair in 1905 when it celebrated the one hundreth centenary of its Nottingham connection. *(Nottingham Markets and Fairs Department)*

14. The first visit of the Cake Walk to Nottingham in 1908. It was owned by A. Richards of Hull seen on the front and a poster on it tells us that it had come direct from Fun City at Olympia. The ride consisted of a number of oscillating platforms and the name was derived from a Negro Dance. The steam wagon is Foden No. 7141 and it was adapted for fairground use with a generator mounted on the front end of the boiler. In the background is Bostock and Wombwell's menagerie. *(Nottingham Markets and Fairs Department)*

15. **The scene in 1910 with Reuben Holdsworth's Flying Pigs and Balloons in the centre.**
(Nottingham Markets and Fairs Department)

16. **The Goose Fair scene in 1908. An interesting point is that Collin's Looping the Loop Motors in left foreground had to be built up to accommodate the lamp post inside the catwalk. The Flying Pigs can be seen on the right foreground.**
(Anne Russon)

17. **The scene at dusk at the 1909 fair, again showing the Looping the Loop Motors but with a Razzle Dazzle in centre. Illumination was provided by a multitude of arc lamps and naptha flares.**
(Anne Russon)

18. The first visit of the Big Wheel to the Goose Fair was in 1907 and seven years later, in 1914 it can be seen how the much condemned rides had taken over. *(Nottingham Markets and Fairs Department)*

19. The 1910 fair and among the shows is President Kemp's Bioscope obviously impressing the punter with 'Our Navy Prepared For War'. Next door is John Proctor's bioscope. *(Nottingham Markets and Fairs Department)*

20. The shows in front of the old Exchange in 1908. Here is President Kemp's 'Theatre Unique' again and John Proctor's Bioscope showing 'The Wigan Colliery Disaster' and 'A Race With Death'. ***(Nottingham Markets and Fairs Department)***

21. The Helter Skelter is one of the oldest fairground attractions and in this Goose Fair photograph it carries the appropriate message, 'Slip the Slip to Cure the Pip' at 1d per ride. ***(Nottingham Markets and Fairs Department)***

22. The new Council House takes shape in place of the old Exchange in 1927, for the last Goose Fair on the Great Market Place. Pat Collin's Whale Island Scenic ride is on the left with his Dragons on the right. Behind are the Ashley Gallopers, well known on the old and new sites.
(Nottingham Markets and Fairs Department)

23. Looking down on a later Goose Fair on the Forest Site.
(Nottingham Markets and Fairs Department)

CHAPTER THREE
SHOWS

Travelling shows were the foundation stone of the amusement fairs and the earliest of them, the theatre booths, entertained the public for decades before even the first humble roundabout was thought of. By an eighteenth century licence system, stage plays could only be performed with the approval of the Lord Chamberlain, approval that was usually given only to theatres with a Royal Charter and which saw the London fairground scene dominated by the booths which could obtain occasional licences for the duration of a fair.

The famous names of the stage could also be found on the fairground. The great Garrick appeared in the booths. Henry Fielding was on the fairground for about nine years, producing the 'The Beggar's Opera' only a few months after its London theatre presentation and bringing a fashionable audience to the fair. It was Henry Fielding who left an impression of what life was like for the actor-managers. '..........a valuable actor must sleep in the pit, wake early to sweep the theatre and throw new sawdust into the boxes. He must teach the dull ones how to act and rout up the idlers from the straw. When the fair begins he should walk round the stage showing off his dress, dance with his fellows, sing, laugh and joke with the crowd, keeping them merry and making sure they come in. Sometimes he should dress normally and go into the crowd and shout as a stranger at the magnificence of his own booth, a good trick that never fails to make an audience, then he has only to slip away, dress in costume and mount the stage to strum and dance, sing and trumpet and roar over again.'

In addition to the actors, the eighteenth century fairground scene was a home for fire eaters, bell ringers, jugglers, acrobats, known as 'tumblers' at this period, and magicians.

This patronage by society, and Samual Pepys was among those who travelled from London to Cambridge for Stourbridge fair, did not last. The reduction of Bartholomew Fair from two weeks to three days in 1750 drove the best actors from the booths. It was no longer worth their while, and they took the fashionable audiences with them.

Fairs generally were becoming the province of the working class. Far from starting a decline, however, the shows grew in size. Richardson's huge theatre adapted to the travelling life offering farce, spectacle and melodrama. The Paragon Theatre would stay in Nottingham for many weeks after Goose Fair, using any available piece of land for a short stay in each suburb. At Christmas they would present pantomime with local children being given the chance to 'tread the boards' as extras.

Wombwell created the travelling menagerie and it was not long before no fair was complete without its animal show. There were Mander's, Hilton's, Bostock's, Chipperfield's, Atkins', Sedgewick's, and Ballard's, which achieved fame in 1816 when a lioness escaped and attacked a horse of the Exeter Mail. It was the answer to a showman's dream, the public readily paid extra to see such a notorious animal.

Fairs provided early homes for the small tenting circuses. These were modest affairs and rarely had more than three or four horses. Horses plus cast performed on a stage outside between shows to attract the public in. The horses stood in a row while the acrobats demonstrated the skills of their trade, a clown amused the crowds with wisecracks, while the owner took to the big drum, encouraging onlookers to fill his circus tent. Only when they had a full house would the show begin. Performances were short, a display of horsemanship, tight rope walking and acrobatics and then it was time to start again on the outside stage. It was hard work for everyone concerned. From noon to midnight they would be on stage, attracting the public as long as there was a chance of packing them inside.

Although the life was hard opportunities were there. The self styled 'Lord' George Sanger moved into circus by buying a horse and pony. This was trained to do such diverse acts as 'fortune telling' and 'card picking', and the horse was taught to gallop in a circus manner round the ring. A clown and other artistes were recruited for a season that began at King's Lynn. Such was his success that he was soon able to enlarge the circus. His takings after a stay in Manchester gave him the opportunity to buy nine more horses and two ponies. And the circus was so popular during a tour of Scotland that Sanger was able to double the admission charge of one penny and three pence, and on occasions even charged two shillings! From these humble beginnings George Sanger progressed until, at the height of his success, he was travelling with a train of over sixty vehicles. Ten wagons carried the tent and seating, a score or more wagons were reserved for the animals, there were wagons for foals, property and wardrobe. A portable blacksmith's forge travelled with them and then there were the living wagons, a harness wagon, tableau wagons and the massive band wagon. More than one hundred and fifty sturdy horses were needed, while the circus horses were tethered behind the wagons. The slower moving elephants and camels would be sent on ahead. The permanent staff included performers, bandsmen, grooms, tentmen, veterinary surgeons, riding up and down the line on ponies looking after the animals, wheelwrights, saddle and harness makers, blacksmiths, carpenters, animal keepers, messmen, and office staff, all part of what could be a two mile convoy that received a rapturous welcome wherever it passed through.

Peep shows that began as humble boxes on four legs but progressed into a full size booth with trumpet barrel organ, numerous viewpoints, optic lenses and changing, candle lit, painted backcloths, approaching as near as possible the magic lantern which was to replace it, giving both glimpses of history as well as anticipating events of the time, arrived on the fairground

At fairs large and small, Marionette Shows entertained young and old. Such was their popularity that one authority on the subject has checked 117 different troupes travelling the country between 1800 and the outbreak of the First World War. Most were family shows, handed down from father to son, and one of the most famous of these families must have been the Tillers, for no less than five branches of the family travelled their marionette shows. Fortunately, one of the last, 'Tiller's Royal Marionette Show' has survived into preservation at the Rutland Cottage Music and Fair Museum at Whaplode St Catherines, near Spalding, Lincs. Here is the cast for the ballet 'Coppelia', the pantomime 'Babes in the Wood' and many of the one penny plays that provided much of their material. Altogether Ray and Iris Tunnicliff have collected 22 of the actual figures, eight original backgrounds, side scenery and a stage, enough, in fact, for the marionettes to actually be travelled. The show, which is said to have gained its 'Royal' prefix after entertaining the children of Queen Victoria in Hyde Park, although there is no real proof of this, has a strong Lincolnshire connection.

When the First World War started this branch of the Tiller

family was touring the county, performing at the time at Long Sutton. When a prohibition on East Coast travel was declared, they had no alternative but to settle down in the village where Jimmy Tiller, now well into his nineties, still lives. He began with the marionettes at the age of six years, brought in to help his mother, father and three brothers work the figures on their nine feet high strings. He was a distinctive figure as a youngster, wearing a red hat with a bobble knitted by his mother so she could easily find her son among the masses that flocked the fairground whenever the travelling showmen appeared. There were many moments of light relief for both operators and audiences. On one occasion young Jimmy was standing at the rear of the stage waiting to operate a marionette representing a sick child with the line 'Oh father, am I going to die?' Then as his moment arrived, the youngster, tired after a play period with friends, fell asleep. His father jolted him back to reality so hard that the red hat fell off, dropping over the figure he was controlling. He spoke his line almost automatically but the audience were laughing too much for all but a few to hear his father's response, 'I'll guarantee it if you fall asleep again.'

If this had taken place in the seventeenth or eighteenth centuries, however, the family would have been prosecuted. For then the puppets were not allowed to have voices as a showman discovered at London's Bartholomew Fair in 1797 when he was prosecuted for presenting his puppets in satirical dialogue.

The fairground was a hard school for youngsters like Jimmy Tiller. Although he was taught to play the piano by an accomplished muscian, there was no allowance for youth during an actual performance. His father accompanied him on the violin when they were out on the front of the stage entertaining the public and enticing them into the show. He listened to every note his son played and even a slight mistake brought a painful clip across the knuckles from the violin bow.

In the smaller villages the marionettes took the place of the large theatre companies who would not have found it worthwhile to attend. For here were those same plays but acted out by the puppet figures. No script was needed for the comedy that usually began their shows for Jimmy Tiller can still remember the two village idiots with their donkey and loaded cart marionettes. The scene as acted out shows a donkey that sits down and refuses to move whatever the two figures do. When they are desperate to continue, the devil appears. He offers help in return for half of a box marked 'fresh bloaters' on the cart. The villagers accept the offer, but when the donkey had been persuaded to move by the devil, they go back on their word, moving off, laughing at the way they have tricked him. At that moment the box, expertly worked by the Tiller family, changes into a dragon which chases the luckless pair who are seen running for their lives as the curtain comes down.

Initially the marionette show, with some figures Jimmy Tiller has checked back to eighteenth century Italian craftsmen, was even larger than one operated by his father and family. For following the death of his grandfather, the show was split between Jimmy's father and his aunt. She travelled for many years as the Excelsior Marionettes while Jimmy's side used that 'Royal' prefix. Like many other shows, Tiller's Royal Marionettes were totally dependant on horses, although they never owned one of their own. Each time they moved on, they would negotiate with a local farmer for the hire of horses to move living van and show to the next village or fair. This way they avoided having to feed the animals and find stable and grazing facilities.

Of all the shows performed on the fairground, however, it was the Ghost Shows that caused the greatest sensation. Although most people who visited these at fairs throughout the country knew that there be no such things as ghosts, they remained baffled on the appearance of that 'apparition'. The Polytechnic in London's Regent Street was the setting in 1863 for Professor Pepper's astonishing introduction of what he called 'Pepper's Ghost Illusion'. Inevitably when news of the show spread to the fairgrounds, showmen mingled with the large public audiences. But rather than be there for thrills and amazement, they were searching for the backroom secrets that would unlock large financial riches.

To the audiences the Ghost Show stage looked like any other in a travelling show. But it was not. For fixed at an angle of 45 degrees was a large sheet of plate glass on which the ghostly figures appeared.

With the careful arrangement of stage curtains, the glass was invisible to an amazed audience that saw 'ghost' figures appear amongst the real actors. Beneath the glass was another stage known to the actors as 'the oven'. However, the only time they were seen by the paying public was when the bright lights they performed in front of reflected their images onto the angled glass and hence onto the stage proper. Light and reflection were the secret of the illusion and it was not long before shrewd showmen had worked this out and 'Ghost Shows' were proving to be good money earners in towns and villages all over the country. Spine chilling illusions were possible and the finale often used the illusion to its maximum, ghosts and hobgoblins filling a darkened church yard, appearing from behind almost every tombstone, sending a captivated audience home through darkened streets with many an anxious glance over their shoulders.

The shows catered for all tastes and both human tableaux and wax imitations played their part in bringing both popular drama and history to an amazed public. Mander's Royal Moving Waxworks delighted audiences everywhere with its life sized mechanical figures in their superb costumes. This was a large show with a 'walk up' front and the fine array of wax tableaux exhibited in box waggons drawn into a square to form the booth. The limbs were made to move by a series of wheels and pulleys operated by men who were out of sight of the audience. A lecturer described each of the tableau in detail, and there can be little doubt that the peak of his ororaty skills were reached when an astonished audience gazed in awe at the star exhibit, 'The Last Supper'.

While the entertainments at small country fairs would be mere echoes of those gathered at the major events, they met a social need unknown in the towns. It was a unique annual occasion, the one break in an otherwise ever ongoing life of servitude.

Those working away from their home village would return for the festivities, where a royal welcome would await them. The women folk 'scrubbed and polished' and generally 'rightled' their homes in preparation for these family reunions. Kitchens were hot with the baking of pies, tarts and cakes, and specialites of the region, such as Lincolnshire chine, pieces of bacon scored and stuffed with a parsley mixture and then boiled, were there to cut and cut again.

The greatest excitement centred on the fair. There would be gingerbread and toys to buy, swings, peep shows, marionettes and Punch and Judy. The professional entertainers would be supplemented by the sports of the community, everything from horse and foot racing to all in wrestling, and it was at these fairs that the showmen spent the greater part of their year.

If, however, these were the occasions for release from rural servitude, for the showmen they were a part of their own particular servitude.

24. Girls stand in front of a Kie or Wild Man Show in the West Country. Date and location are unknown. *(Author)*

25. Will Hardy travelled a Ghost Illusion Show, Wax Works and Theatre in the Leicestershire area. *(Author)*

26. The realism of the Wax Works was complete as this picture illustrates. Will Hardy is on the right with his daughter. A relative is in the pay box and the person on the far left is another relative. The rest are waxworks. *(Author)*

27. Jimmy Tiller, now in his nineties, demonstrates the art of working the marionette. *(Author)*

28. The Devil and one of the village idiots now at the Rutland Cottage Music and Fair Museum. *(Author)*

29. The mule and cart from the sketch also in the museum. *(Author)*

30. Another example from the Rutland Cottage Music and Fair Museum of the skills of the operator can be seen in this three headed figure that Jimmy Tiller and his family used to operate. *(Author)*

31. Whiting's Coconut sheet at Chesterfield in the thirties. J. Whiting is on the left. ***(Nottingham Markets Department)***

32. An early sidestall showing Henry Redfern with his 'Uptodate New Games of Skill'. ***(Rennie Crick)***

33. An unidentified round stall dating from about 1910 and with the females posing for a photograph. ***(Rennie Crick)***

34. Tom Norman's Travelling Palladium show was a popular event wherever it attended. He was known as the 'Silver King' and made many broadcasts about fairground matters. One of his famous attractions included Tommy Jackson, the armless pianist who attracted considerable media attention. The twin bells on the show front were always borrowed to open Goose Fair. The bells were ultimately given to the city and are still used by the Lord Mayor as he commences the merrymaking each year. *(Author)*

35. Pepper's Ghost Illusion was also toured by travelling acting companies as this 1892 poster shows.
(Rutland Cottage Music and Fairground Museum)

CHAPTER FOUR

THE SHOWMEN

'Lord' George Sanger spent his formative years living and travelling in a horse drawn van twelve feet by seven by seven with his father, mother, brother and sister. But possibly he considered himself fortunate when compared with his father's life during the Napoleonic Wars.

A native of Wiltshire where he was a qualified toolmaker, Sanger's father was pressganged into the Royal Navy during a visit to London. Wounded during the Battle of Trafalgar he returned home with just a ten pounds a year pension. His parents had died during his enforced ten years at sea and with no other way of making a living, he put to good use tricks he had learned from two conjurers, like himself pressed into the navy, starting as a showman at Bristol Fair.

While many of the smaller show owners saw a horse and living van as the height of luxury, committed as they were to travelling everywhere on foot with any tools of the trade, even with a horse and van life was far from easy. The Sanger family were inside when their van overturned during the infamous 'Battle of the Oxford Road' near Reading in 1833.

These were the days before Guild Rules and booked space at fairs. It was a case of every man for himself and the best positions went to the early arrivals. A race from Reading's May Day Fair to Henley's Fair, held on May 3rd, began between the drivers of Hilton's and Wombwell's Menageries, both intent on arriving first and claiming the best position. Wombwell was first away, but closely followed by Hilton. Wombwell's larger menagerie was the slower moving and a few miles out of Reading, Hilton tried to overtake. Wombwell's men took preventative action, pulling the wagons across the road. A Hilton man knocked a Wombwell man off a wagon with a tent pole and battle was on. The weapons were tent poles, whips and crowbars and the troops included three giants, an armless man who normally painted pictures with his feet, a living skeleton and Wombwell's 'Fat Tom', said to be the heaviest man in the country. Although there was no loss of life, Reading hospital had a hectic time dealing with the injured.

While such outbreaks of fairground rivalry were small, night time travel on the roads of Victorian England could be a frightening experience. The days of the highwaymen may have been over, but gangs of footpads were common enough to make most wary of travelling alone at night. And while body snatchers were the worst that the Sangster family encountered, few would venture out in the dark, if they were by themselves and unarmed.

Fairgrounds were regarded with suspicion by the authorities. And if the showmen were not themselves regarded as criminals, they were seen as the attraction that brought criminals into a locality, fair followers that soon brought the show people into general disrepute. However, the criminal element who followed the fair were an embarrassment to genuine showmen for the damage they did to his reputation among communities that he needed to visit each year in the course of business.

There is little doubt that there were fracas when the fairs were in town or village, but often they were started after the amusements had closed down and sometimes directed at the showmen themselves. Even then they were fortunate if they could prove they were the injured party. George Sanger's father once found himself facing imprisonment for defending his wagon and family against a violent mob with a blunderbuss loaded with marbles.

That great City of London fair, Bartholomew's, which took its origin at the time of the founding of St. Bartholomew's Priory, Hospital and Church in 1102, by Raphere, the king's jester, was cut to a third of its length in the 1750s, as part of the battle against rowdy living. If these early showmen looked on themselves as working class entertainers, their audiences often regarded them as fair game for their own particular violence. In superstitious, isolated rural communities, they were often open to attack just because they were strangers.

The travelling criminal class had an advantage here, they could wear a rural smock and intermingle with the crowds while showmen, by the nature of their business, had to be conspicuous. In some northern mining villages, the men going on shift saw in the showmen a chance to prove their strength. Occasionally the violence got out of hand and at one Cheshire fair, a gingerbread seller was kicked to death by the clogs of local people.

Mere survival was never enough, showmen had to rise above the environment if they were to make a living, but even then it was often a hand to mouth existence. On one occasion the Sanger family found themselves marooned on one side of a toll bridge with insufficient funds to go over. An impromptu show, however, entertaining fellow travellers brought the required 'crossing money' and some to spare.

Ingenuity was the order of the day if success was to come to the family. Lord George Sanger's father had a peep show at the beginning of his career. Not for him, however, such features as the Battle of Trafalgar, at which he was injured. He was an eye witness to a murder during a pub brawl and his own hastily painted sketches of the event proved to be money winners wherever the family travelled.

While life was hard in the extreme with show people thinking nothing of walking twenty miles to a fair the following day, for the true entrepreneurs, the rewards could also be high. Richardson, the theatre owner came into the business as an orphan pot boy with a peep show he inherited from someone he had befriended. When he died he was worth £40,000, and other showmen could claim that their income was such that members of the family helped themselves from the takings as they needed money. Some became rich and stayed rich. Others became rich and found money too big a problem to handle and were soon back where they had started. However, among those who became rich and stayed rich, were the foundations of the great show families of today, including that of Pat Collins.

He was born in Chester in 1859 and had two brothers, John and Michael and two sisters, Maggie and Johanna. Like many other well known showmen, he ran away from home at the age of eight years to join his Irish father who had settled in Chester. There he turned the handle of the organ in the centre of the 'push round dobbies'. In an interview with a Nottingham newspaper reporter, in 1897, Pat Collins recalled how he had started on his own sixteen years before, presenting a small set of roundabouts, some swings and a shooter. By the time of the interview he had two sets of Gondolas, a bicycle ride, one set of switchback ponies, two sets of jumping horses, a channel tunnel railway, a set of platform gallopers, two menageries and two whole fairs of smaller attractions. And he could claim to be the pioneer of all roundabouts except the roly-poly. He was providing employment for between 400 and 500 workmen including joiners, carpenters, painters, blacksmiths and electricians. He had his own works at Walsall and such was his eye for aesthetic beauty that he could get through 400 pounds of gold leaf during the winter maintenance months.

Pat Collins was not the first showman to run away from home for a life on the fairs. David Miller was another 'runaway' who joined the travelling fraternity after a night in an ale house where monies intended for other purposes disappeared. And to the dismay of his parents, William Taylor's father decided the fair was the place to exhibit his 7 ft 8 in frame as 'The Ilkeston Giant'. Ultimately, of course, this gave us the famed William Taylor Bioscope Shows.

Entertainment for some, however, was in the blood, as 'Master Showman' George Aspland showed. He was born at Holbeach in 1836, beginning his working life as an errand boy to Mr Snare, the Ironmonger. He then turned to bakery before working in agriculture, but from an early age he became interested in entertaining his neighbours. Shooting was second nature to most Fen folk and this budding showman decided to give everyone a chance to take part in the sport. His first home-made 'shooter' was somewhat crude, consisting of only a whitewashed iron target in a roped off area. There was an attendant with a whitewash brush at the rear and he re-brushed the target after every 'go'. It is believed that the shooter made its debut on the Holbeach cricket field and such was the success that George Aspland decided to have a season at nearby Skegness with it.

At this time, the 1850s, the Volunteer Army had been formed in Britain and efficient rifles were beginning to be produced, popularising the sport of target shooting. Showmen soon appreciated that here was another attraction to go along with the various throwing games that were a part of every fair. The tube shooter was the showman's answer for the fairground. Initially the punters fired along a single tube set up behind an ornamental front. This soon developed into the gallery wagon. The 26 foot long tubes, with a target enclosed in a steel box containing a backstop, telescope together for travelling and pass from side to side through the wagon, one under the bed and the other under the table. It was not long before George Aspland had replaced his home-built shooter for one of these attractive newcomers.

Ever the pioneer, it was not long before he added a photographic booth and as well as doing the camera work, did his own developing and printing.

It was in 1872 at Boston, by then his 'home' town, that George Aspland introduced the fairground visitor to what was the rage of the rich, bicycling. His Velocipide ride consisted of a set of bicycles ridden by his customers round a metal track. There were problems, however, particularly when it came to imposing a braking effect against the combined power of the cyclists, and it required great effort to restrict the period of the ride.

This Lincolnshire showman's progression continued when he presented his first roundabout at Boston that same year and six years later the 'Sea on Land', those rolling boats that were a revolutionary introduction. George Aspland seized every opportunity and through presenting an amusement-starved public with the thrills they demanded, built up from that home-built 'shooter' one of the leading fairground businesses with Galloping Horse Roundabouts, a Savage-built prototype switchback and scenic rides. In 1875 George Aspland had been joined by his brother-in-law, Ben Howden, a talented engineer who was responsible for much of the innovative work that became associated with Aspland and Howden. Ben Howden first managed the business, but took it over when George Aspland died in 1911. However, it was four years earlier that he took the step that was to dictate the future of the family by buying their first 'talking picture' or bioscope show.

Their fairground circuit, like many others in East Anglia started at King's Lynn, progressed to Wisbech, Stamford, Norwich, Yarmouth, Lincoln and Boston. Then it was time for the Whit fair at York and the summer was spent touring through what was then the West Riding of Yorkshire. Like other fairground families connected with those early travelling cinemas, the Aspland-Howden's settled down into a permanent cinema building, laying the foundation for Boston's cinema industry.

George Wombwell came into the business in 1807 and showed the truth in that saying 'great oaks from little acorns grow'. Wombwell, a Soho shoemaker had always been fascinated by animals. At the age of twenty seven, he bought a pair of boa-constrictors for £75 and as a side line exhibited them in his shop. Such was the response from an amazed public eager to view some of the first such snakes to arrive in this country that within three weeks he had realised considerably more than their cost. As a writer of the time recalled, 'Stimulated by the success thus achieved, he commenced his caravan journeys throughout the United Kingdom, visiting all the great fairs, adding all the time to his menageries of animals. When he died in 1850, Wombwell was a wealthy man with three huge menageries which travelled in different parts of the country. The largest, with which he himself always travelled, consisted of over forty wagons. And among the magnificent collection of animals were many bred and reared by the proprietor himself.'

In his travelling career George Wombwell had never been known to miss London's Bartholomew's fair. However, on one occasion when his No.1 Menagerie was at Newcastle Fair, a fortnight's travel from the city, he decided to give 'Bartlemy Fair' a miss. Then, ten days before the event, news came in that his rival, Atkins' was advertising 'the only wild beast show at the fair', Wombwell decided to act.

After an almost non stop journey he reached London on the morning of the fair. The cost, however, was great. His elephant, the favourite among the many animals, died from exertion. Immediately Atkins advertised 'the only live elephant at the fair'. Wombwell responded by announcing 'the only dead elephant at the fair'. And the public responded in style. They had seen many live elephants but the chance to see and get near a dead elephant was something not to be missed!

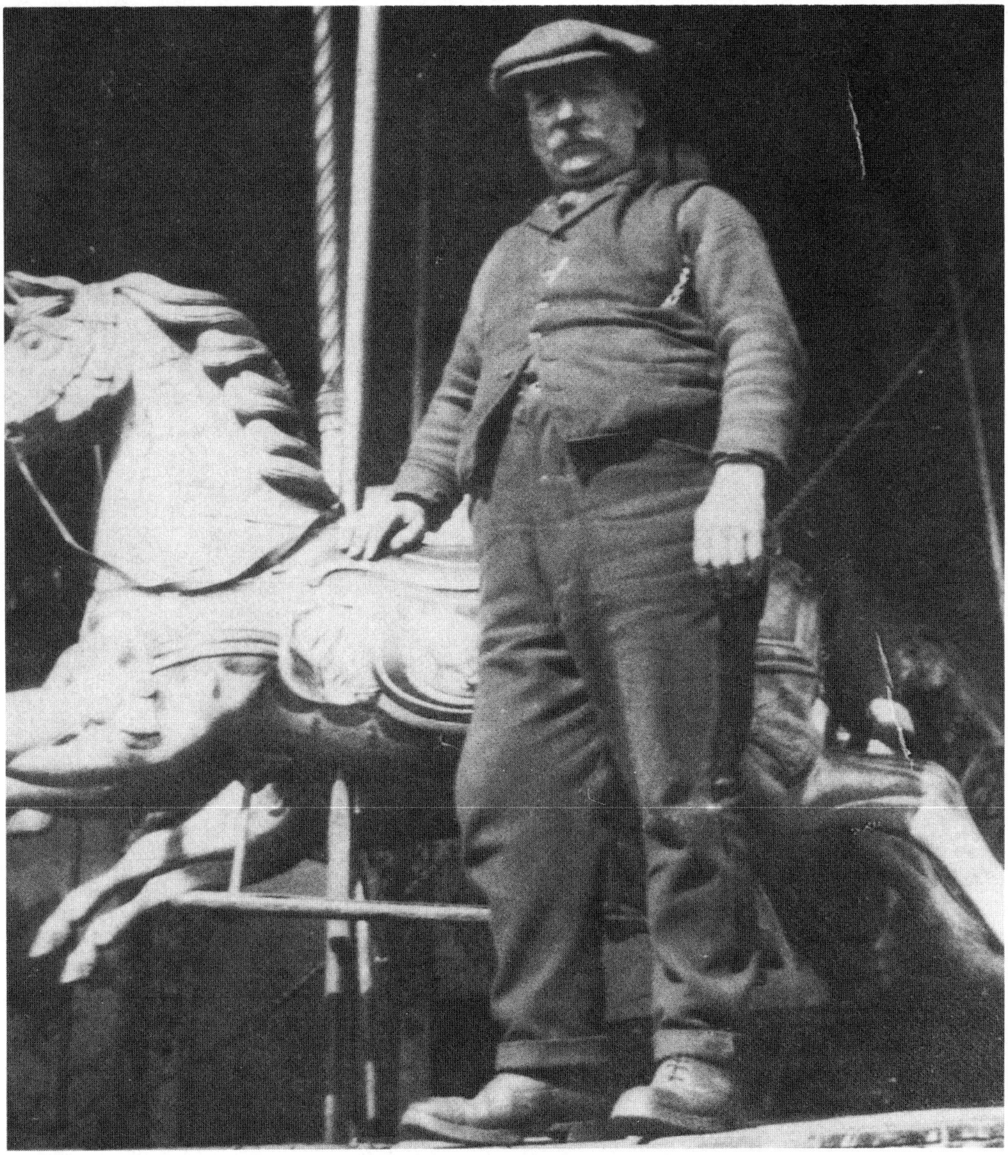

36. Travelling fairs appear to have been the mecca for postcard photographers. Here Laurie Crick poses for the camera on his three abreast.
(Rennie Crick)

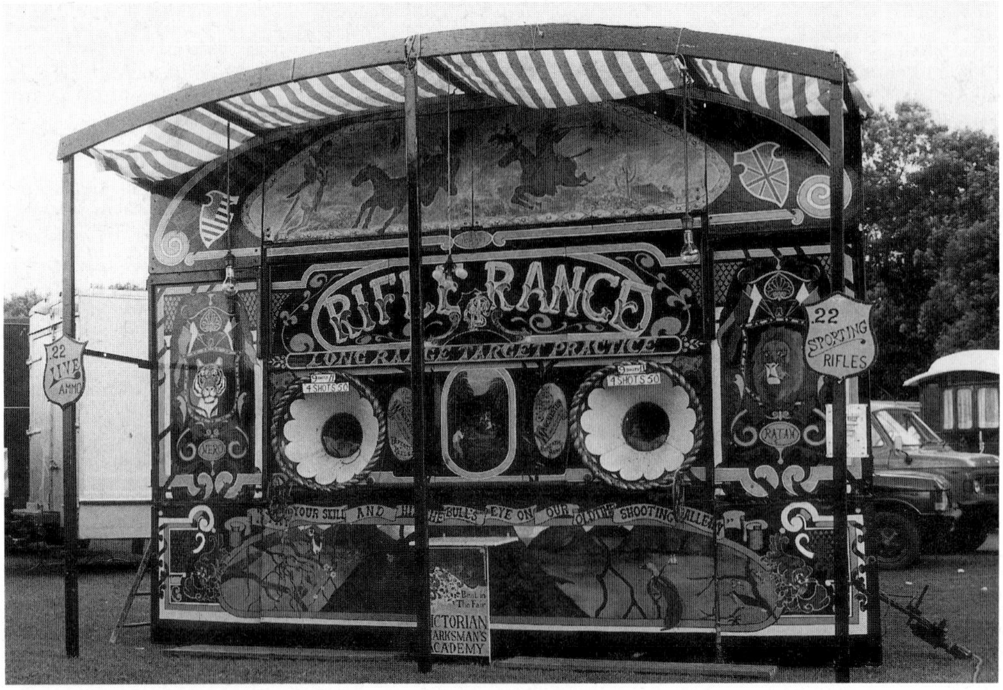

37. The Tube Shooter gave George Aspland a boost in his then new career. This one is in preservation and is owned by P. Swindlehurst of Leek.
(Author)

38. Showing the rear of a tube shooter.
(Author)

39. Looking down on the fair in George Aspland's adopted town of Boston showing the crowds outside Aspland's show.
(Author)

40. Groups pose for the camera on the front of Aspland's Mammoth Exhibition.
(Rutland Cottage Music and Fairground Museum)

41. From a start with a home-made shooter, George Aspland progressed until he was able to offer the famed Aspland's Switchback which is now in the Cushing collection.
(Rutland Cottage Music and Fair Museum)

42. A Barker and Farrar family group taken at an unknown fairground location.
(Author)

43. An interesting but unfortunately unidentified photograph of sailors from many ships in the Royal Navy circa the First World War. Obviously taken on Anderton and Rowlands Racing Motors and with the notice that all the staff have joined the colours, could this be a group photograph of the patriotism shown by everyone connected with the fairground?
(Author)

44. A group of old time showmen taken at the Goose Fair. From left to right, back row: Tom Norman, Walter Green, Joe Ling, W. Croydon, Frank Harniess, A. Dick, J.R. Styles. Front Row: Pat Collins, F. Coope, John Collins, F. Bostock, Geo. C.A. Austin. *(Nottingham Markets and Fairs Department)*

45. An early caravan belonging to Billy Foreshaw, a Lancashire showman. *(Rennie Crick)*

CHAPTER FIVE

THE GUILD

Fairgrounds are a colourful part of our national heritage. Their glitter and tinsel brings pleasure to young and old, and it is their proud boast that in town and country the fairground is the last bastion of true family entertainment. Yet almost a century ago, if one man could have influenced Parliamentary voting, the show people might have been part of our magnificent past.

For George Smith, Member of Parliament for Coalville, Leicestershire, who had been active in promoting Bills relating to migratory workers, decided to turn his attentions to the fairground. If his Private Members' Bill had passed through the House of Commons, restrictive legislation could have forced their mobile living wagons off the road. Not only did he propose statutory inspection and registration of the wagons, but that the inspecting body, the local authority, would be able to change the requirements and fees charged without any reference back to Parliament.

For once the individuality of the fairground scene was forgotten and in 1889 the Black Lion Hotel at Salford played host to a gathering of the leading figures in the business. Men such as 'Lord' George Sanger, Pat Collins, J.W. Bostock of menagerie fame, the Studts of Wales, McIndoes of Scotland and the Murphy family from the North-East, all rallied to save the fairground. George Smith himself spoke to the meeting; while no actual harm came to him, he is said to have left hurriedly by a rear entrance! The outcome was the United Kingdom Showmen and Van Dwellers Association, which was not only to defeat the proposed legislation, but give us the fairground we know today. However, one of the leading figures, in what was to be a long but successful struggle, was an outsider, the Rev. Thomas Horne, a curate from Rotherham.

In the beginning he felt sympathy for the cause, but as he came into contact with more and more showmen, the Rev Horne became completely immersed in their interests. He organised a mission and travelled more than 10,000 miles a year round the fairgrounds of Britain.

Their opponents cause was not helped when health inspectors, sent to make spot checks on showmen, reported that they had rarely seen such healthy people. There must have been those though, including 'Lord' George Sanger, who conveniently forgot about their own experiences in those horse drawn wagons.

When the Association came into being, however, showmen were business people with true integrity. The Queen had seen Sanger's circus, Bostock's menagerie had travelled in Europe, and Pat Collins even circularised his tenants about their personal appearances. By now the investments in fairground rides were considerable and the showmen depended on public goodwill for retaining the sites of the old fairs. However, the Association, of which J. W. Bostock became the first President, was formed to check legislation against van dwellers and had no powers for regulating the day to day running of the fairground. Little of its work concerned the average fairground person and after that initial impetus, it began to lose members.

Ride owners formed the alternative 'British Roundabout Proprietors' and Showman's Union'. However, there were soon accusations of a 'combine' and high rents for the smaller showmen. This seemed to many to be particularly apparent when the Van Dweller's Association and the Proprietors' Union had the same secretary. In 1910, during the period when 'Lord' George Sanger was at the helm the title, 'Showman's Guild of Great Britain' was adopted as more descriptive of the aims and ideals of the organisation.

Those aims, today as yesterday, are the protection of members' livelihoods through a strictly enforced code of conduct and through the legal and constitutional process of the country. Each of its 5,000 members has equal status regardless of the size of their businesses. Guild rules are enforced by disciplinary tribunals, and as well as regulating the day to day running of fairs, they control every aspect of a member's behaviour. Today, the Guild has ensured that events like the 'Battle of the Oxford Road' are moments of history. The modern fairground, and the positions rides occupy, are strictly controlled through the 'Two Year Rule'. This means that any showman, large or small, who has occupied a site for the previous two years has first call on that site in succeeding years.

Showmen see this as the 'Backbone of the Guild', ensuring the survival of smaller members against the more wealthy ride owners who could outbid for a prime site. Where a fair site is leased by a Guild member, he can only sub-let to other members, and the rents must remain the same each year, unless the ground owner has demanded more. Even when a fair is organised by the local authority, they are happy to work with the Guild. Although this means that in relation to the 'Two Year Rule' they have little control over the rides booked in, they are sure of the safety factors of the machines and the general conduct of their tenants.

The Guild, more than anyone else, is aware of the inherent dangers on the fairground. They insist on an annual inspection of all rides, carried out by independent engineers, and if they refuse to issue a 'certificate of safety' the owner is prohibited from using the attraction until the engineers are satisfied.

Although on major events, such as the Goose Fair, the two year rule applies, there is still variety in the machines. Some of the positions are floating ones, they have not been allocated for the necessary two years to the same man, so the council decides who is to stand on them and with what. The showmen also know the value of change and the major figures such as Pat Collins will 'ring the changes' in the machines that he brings each year, so that there is always something different to attract the public.

To watch the annual pull-on of a major fair is to appreciate that now, as in the past, one of the most important possessions of every travelling family is their living wagon. Today, however, they are mobile homes in the true sense of the word, with fitted kitchens, bathrooms with showers, and living areas with every comfort from storage heaters to television and video.

During the travelling season home is where the work is, but during the winter they return to their permanent bases. This is the time for maintenance on the rides and for the children to receive their formal education, for while during the travelling season they learn the self sufficiency needed for their profession; skills as carpentry, electricity and painting, then motor mechanics, business management and accountancy.

But more than anything, the season is the time they make contact with their community. Showmen have a great social awareness. One of their latest campaigns is a 'Say No to Drugs and Strangers' scheme. Fairgrounds carry warning messages, and during the winter months many talk about their lives to children, making this another occasion to warn their audiences of the inherent dangers that exist today.

The Guild, which ensures that all members have an equal status, is accepted at both national and local levels as the negotiating body for the travelling showmen, and has its own parliamentary agent. Within its structure are ten regions covering all of Great Britain. The sections are controlled by a committee elected annually by secret ballot, and four members are appointed to serve on the Central Council. Some of the Central Council's powers have been delegated to the Management, Appeals and Safety Committees.

The first of these deals with financial affairs, the second with disputes between members or sections and the third fairground safety. A high value is placed on this by the Guild and they co-operate closely with the Government's Health and Safety Executive in drawing up a code of safe conduct at fairs.

The showman's bible is *The World's Fair,* a weekly trade paper devoted to fairground activities. Its mainly freelance reporters cover most fairs, recording details of equipment and families present. This is a much valued service enabling the travelling fraternity to keep up to date with the whereabouts of other showmen. Guild notices are published in it as well as advertisements relating to all aspects of a showman's life: ground to let, sales, equipment wanted, personal notices, birthdays, births, deaths as well as 'In Memoriam' tributes.

The paper, started in 1904 by Frank Mellor, the great uncle of the present chairman, Michael Mellor, is indispensable to the travelling fraternity. The true profession of the founder was as a salesman for the lamps and water cans the family firm made for fairground use. Inevitably, as he travelled from fair to fair, he became a messenger, providing his customers with news of fairs and those attending. He soon realised the need for a newspaper and in the beginning produced a single sheet, printed on one side only. From that humble beginning came the showman's official trade paper that now also represents the market industry and the coin slot trade.

The fair, however, is not a classless society. The upper class are the ride owners and the natural succession here is for the elder son to take over the ride on the death of his father and look after his mother and unmarried sisters. To retain the family in their accustomed roles, it is usual for the head of the family to ensure that there are sufficient rides to pass onto all sons. These would be the traditional gift from father to son, although the younger ones may have to move on and find sites of their own. If there were just daughters, arrangements would be made for suitable boys to carry on the business with them, and chosen from the same class.

The middle class in the fairground are the smaller rides owners or those who have juvenile rides or food stalls. These people hardly ever arrange or organise a fair, this is the prerogative of the ride owners, who have the necessary financial resources.

There is a class need on the mart. The upper ride and organising class need the middle class to fill their fairground places, and the middle class, in their turn, need the upper class for the sites on which they can make a living.

The third class are the families who have no large or juvenile rides but provide the fairground with its round and side stalls. Their problems are greater than the others in that while the stalls may make them a living, there is little chance for them to earn the finance required to buy an actual ride. And if they do succeed in buying one, they have to work hard to find a run of sites that can accommodate the ride.

Because of the itinerant nature of the profession, there are other problems. If they register their children in local schools, it is often a case that they are allowed to pass their time in some non-learning capacity, and even if they are absorbed into a class, the stay is so short that the educational value is short. On the plus side, such is the family bond that crime within the community by the community is virtually unknown. Divorce is equally rare, the family unit is the centre of their existence and few husbands would make a major decision without the approval of his wife.

The community spirit of the travelling families can be seen to the full during the winter months when the showmen's own social organisations, based on the Guild areas, run a variety of functions and sporting events.

Showpeople also play a valued part in their local communities. Many belong to voluntary organisations such as the Round Table while others serve as elected members of local councils. There has always been a strong tradition of service to the communities they regard as their homes. Pat Collins became not only Mayor of Walsall but also its Member of Parliament.

The second 'Showman Mayor' was George Thomas Tuby who served Doncaster for many years as Councillor, Alderman and Mayor, as well as holding the office of Guild Vice President. This remarkable man began his career in the fairs with photography and a 'Wo Emma' throwing game. From these small beginings, his business grew until, with seven new Burrell Road Locomotives, he became their second best customer after Pat Collins. His generosity in relation to various charities became legand. In typical showman's style, his progress in local politics was proudly proclaimed by his various Burrell Showmen's engines.

The first was naturally called 'Councillor' to celebrate his election to the council. As his civic career progressed, he had 'Alderman' and 'Mayor'. While there may have been a touch of sadness when 'Ex-Mayor' left Doncaster, throughout its working life it stood as a reminder of the public service that this great showmen did for the town of Doncaster.

46. George Thomas Tuby, the Yorkshire showman, in his Mayoral robes on the occasion of his 70th birthday. ***(Roger Tuby)***

47. On official duty, the Mayor and Mayoress of Doncaster, George Thomas Tuby and Mrs Tuby with Princess Helena Victoria on an official visit to Doncaster in March 1922. ***(Roger Tuby)***

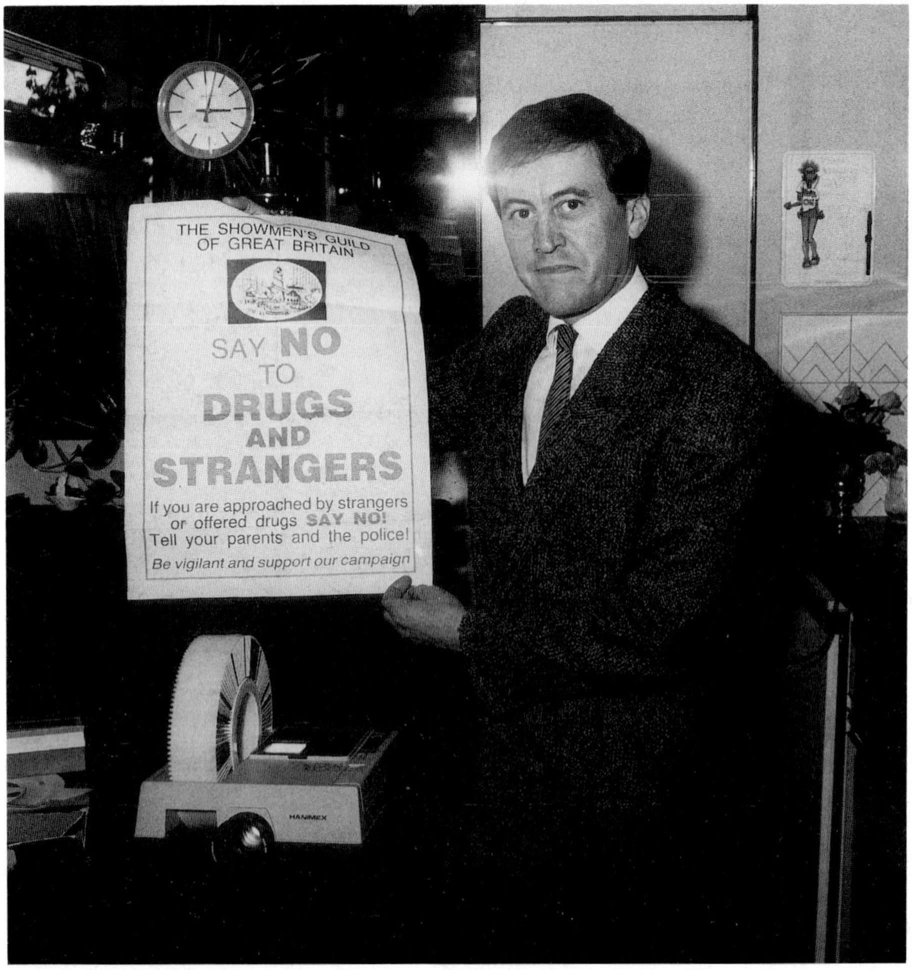

48. Great grandson, Guild member, Roger Tuby demonstrates how he plays his part in the Guild's campaign to warn children of the dangers from drugs and strangers. ***(Author)***

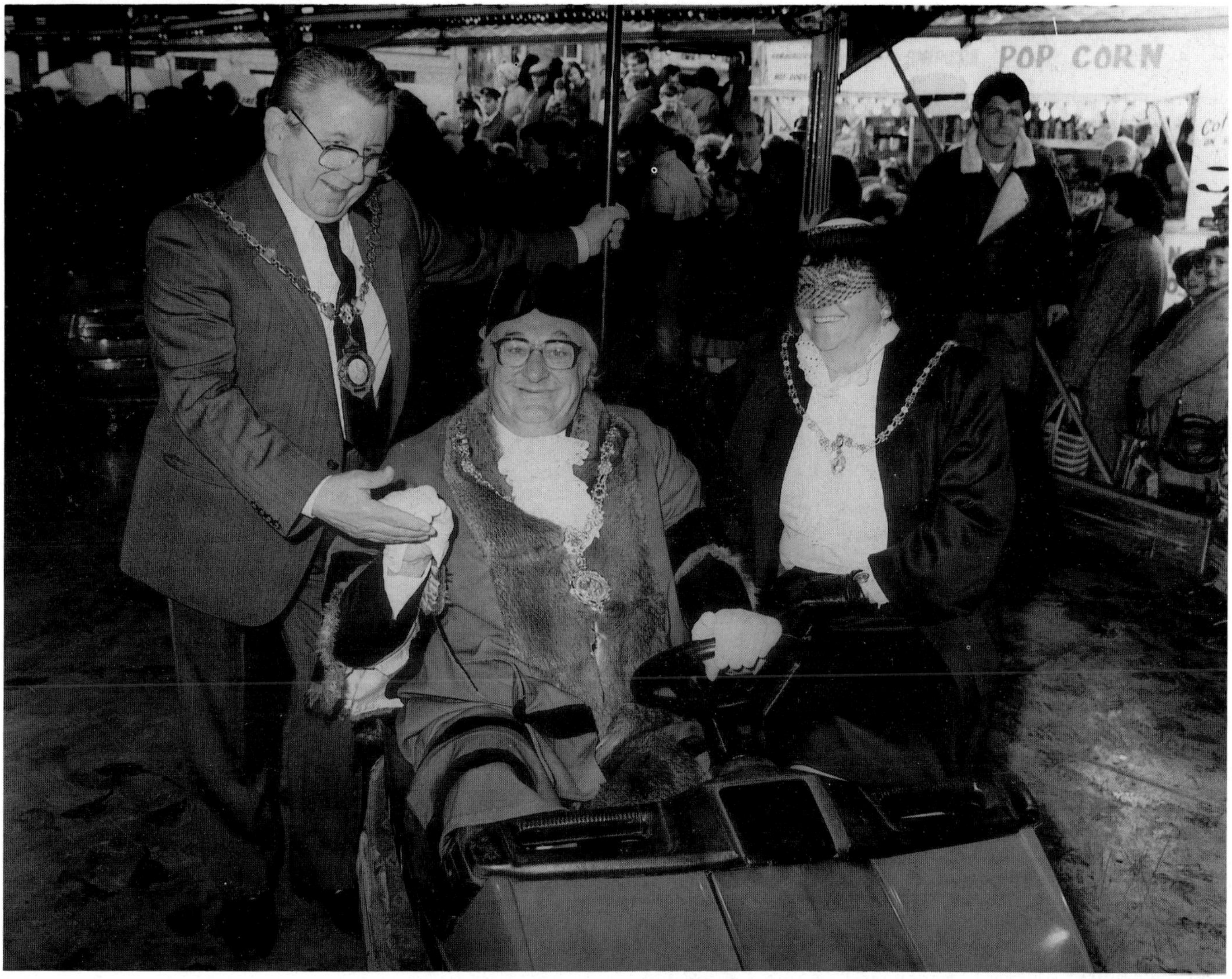

49. Grandson George Thomas Tuby carries on the civic reputation of the family. Mayor of both Whitby and Scarborough, he is seen here in the Scarborough Mayoral robes with the Mayoress, Mrs Anne Tuby, whose father was President of the Showman's Guild, and the Guild President, Harry North at the official opening of Kings Lynn Mart.
(Author)

50. The Guild carry on old traditions and support fully such events as the official opening of King's Lynn Mart, the start of the season for East Anglian showmen.
(Author)

51. A scene in 1924 when taking on water had a different meaning.
(Author)

52. A unique Xmas card from Mr and Mrs Jim Noyce and family.
(Loughborough Markets and Fairs Department)

53. In the yard.
A photograph taken in the 1920s of W. Beach's Switchback cars on truck in their Southall Depot.
(Author)

CHAPTER SIX
BIOSCOPES

For more than two glorious decades the travelling bioscope shows delighted the public. On the fairground, in the first simple 'ground booths' that were later to progress to elaborate 'walk up' shows with massive carved frontages and seating for up to one thousand, the punters of the day were often able to see themselves on the flickering animated pictures that laid the foundation stones for what was to become Britain's film industry.

The story began in London in February, 1896 with the first public showing of the Lumiere brothers 'Cinematographe' at the Marlborough Hall. It was so successful that it was moved to the larger Empire Theatre in Leicester Square, where films of less than a minute's duration became part of the music-hall programme. Delighted audiences flocked to see items such as 'The Blacksmith At Work', 'Bathing In The Mediterranean' and the first ever comedy based on a boy stepping onto a garden hose and releasing the flow of water just as the gardener peered down the hose to trace the stoppage. This success was not lost on showmen. All that was needed to set up a bioscope show was a tent, projector and film and just one year later Randall Monte Williams astonished King's Lynn fairgoers with a display of this new entertainment in just such a portable booth.

Together with his two brothers, Randall Williams was a professional photographer and when they joined up with a firm of scientific engineers, they had the business of taking and showing nicely sewn up. Competition, however, was soon to follow. For that same year William Taylor, whose 7 ft 8 in father had run away to join the fair as the 'Ilkeston Giant', began a bioscope life that was to lead him to the front of the industry. However, there was nothing grand about this fairground film debut. The horse drawn show was nothing more than a 'ground booth', no stage or steps, merely a two wagon frontage with painted canvas fixed to poles above the wagons. There was a Trumpet organ at one side of the central entrance and a Savage electric light engine the other. Naphtha flares were used for outside illumination at night.

At the time of the introduction of the moving pictures, some showmen had a distinct advantage. The Ghost Illusions, Marionette Shows, Waxwork Exhibitions, Menageries etc. were already larger than the 'ground booths' and as they appreciated the potential of this new medium, they were able to show their films in a more ambitious style. Seating was there, and these 'walk ups', so called because customers had to walk up steps to the pay boxes, had ornate frontages and a full length outside stage on which performers could entertain and attract patrons into the film show.

The first silent films had few sub titles and showmen began to employ men of good education as descriptive lecturers, known as 'describers'. They soon developed the ability to bring out the funny patter for comedy and bring their audiences to tears at a time of pathos.

There was no such thing as film hire, and what films were available were purchased outright. Bioscope owners, however, ever aware of the need to involve their audiences, were soon visiting the towns and villages on their route, making films of locals leaving their places of employment. Here was an approach that almost guaranteed a full house. The chance of actually seeing oneself on the screen was a temptation few could resist. Vivid for many months afterwards must have been the memories of sitting in a dark and musty tent on a hard, backless bench, watching pictures that jerked and wobbled through, apparently, a perpetual rainstorm, and shrinking back in alarm at the railway engine that was coming right out of the screen at them.

Sound effects were not long in arriving. It took little imagination for the bioscope owners to appreciate the audience reaction if whistles were blown, rattles shaken, iron rods slammed down and even broken glass thrown about a bucket as two railway locomotives crashed head on.

These crashes were, of course, fake, done in the studio with models. But as the two express locomotives approached closer and closer with the accompanying sound effects, the realism for those early viewers was such that few of the viewing public would have disputed the showman's claim that here was the real thing.

Actuality soon arrived and nothing delighted the public more than the first film combining real scenes with work done in the studio. It featured the Hove Fire Brigade at work, but what made it really sensational was that the fire scenes were tinted a deep red.

Effect workers, however, faced the distinct possibility of the sack in 1906 when the first sound films were introduced. Several bioscope owners went a stage further and installed a device which enabled gramophone records to be used with the picture projector. The intention was for records to be played behind the screen, but unfortunately amplification had not been invented and only the fortunate few in the front seats were aware of the music. In the age of the fairground organ, when half a dozen or so could be playing at once, hearing was a definite problem for everyone on the fairground and it was not long before the gramophone record was discarded.

These fairground pioneers of the cinema faced other problems. In some of the early shows lighting was by Naphtha Flare Lamps, both externally and internally. These consisted of a container holding a gallon of oil and an iron burner heated by a small fire, usually kindled with oily rags and paper. When the burner became hot enough it gave off a bright star shaped light and a number of these lamps strategically positioned provided all the illumination for the shows. The lamps used for interior lighting were often drawn up to the ridge of the booth by means of a rope and pulley, and kept there until the audience were in their places. Before the actual films could be shown, however, the lamps had to be lowered, unhooked and carried outside where they remained burning until they were brought inside for the departure of the audience.

The British Oxygen Company of Statley, Birmingham, provided the steel cylinders of oxygen and hydrogen needed for projection purposes at a price of 4d per cubic foot. These gases formed the 'limelight' used when lighted hydrogen was allowed to touch a lime cone and oxygen was added gradually. There could be a fright for an expectant audience as the lighting was being prepared. For if the oxygen was turned on too fiercely, a rather loud bang would follow as the rubber connecting the gas to the lamp jet was either blown off or burst. This form of illumination was something the entertainment industry adopted after seeing it used externally on such structures as Westminster Bridge.

And while it answered the needs in those early days, it was not without its problems, particularly as the only source of supply was Birmingham. It was difficult for a showman to accurately judge his gas requirements. Business could exceed even optimistic expectations and the weight of the gas cylinders prevented showmen carrying spares in that age of horse transport.

If they were working a long distance from Birmingham it

could mean that the bioscope was out of action for a day or two. For although the company would dispatch requirements on receipt of a telegram, the cylinders had to be sent by passenger train. This could not only mean that the cylinders had to change trains but on occasions stations as well, all adding to the frustration of the showman at the other end. However, with the advent of the portable steam electric light engine from 1891, the carbon burning arc lamp gradually replaced limelight. While this partially removed carriage problems, it also gave an improved illumination and quality of picture.

Electric light engines usually stood on the right hand side of the show front forming part of that frontage. The chimneys were high so that smoke and sparks were carried well clear of the canvas roof that covered the booths. These engines were built into a 'box truck' with heavy iron tyred wheels and this was fitted with shafts for horses to move it from site to site. Often the showmen would send the engine ahead by rail, but there was still a need for horses to move it to and from the station.

The bioscopes became another example of that 'age of achievement' for progressive show owners. William Taylor was one such man and his shows were renowned for their constant improvement. Fronts became more elaborate, a powered Trumpet organ appeared in place of the hand operated one, and with the advent of Savage's portable electric light engines, arc light gradually replaced the naphtha flares. Only five years after that 'ground booth' appeared on the fair, it gave way to a 'walk up' show. Carved panelling replaced the old painted canvas and the Savage electric light engine gave way to a Burrell 8hp D.C.C. No 2497 'Excelsior' which came out of the maker's works on 1st August 1902. It generated the necessary electric power and partly hauled the show.

Further improvements, including cover for the front stage and a new 98 key Marenghi organ to replace the Trumpet organ followed over the next five years, culminating in the arrival of another new Burrell Showman's engine. This was another 8hp D.C.C. No 2898 'Victoria' which left Thetford on 20th April, 1907. Now the show was completely steam hauled. There is little doubt that this was the year that William Taylor reached the peak of his profession, and when he built up his mammoth bioscope that advertised itself as 'The Premier Show Of The Universe', few could doubt that claim.

This Orton and Spooner creation could not only house 1,000 people in red plush seats, it was complete with dummy Royal boxes on each side of the stage. The 120 key Marenghi organ, equivalent to 150 musicians, was 36 feet long and illuminated by 4,000 electric lights which changed colour in time with the music. The organ frontage with entrances on each side was a visual tribute to the craftmanship of carvers and gilders, while above it all were seven illuminated letters, 'TAYLORS' which spelled out a name that had become famous wherever his shows appeared. Even that was not enough, for rather than rest on his laurels William Taylor introduced a form of 'singing and talking pictures'

William Taylor's reputation also came from the crowd-drawing acts who gave a free show on the front stage and then performed before every performance of the bioscope. Dancing girls and comedians were part of the regular staff. For the larger fairs, however, they would be augmented by specially commissioned artists. Trapeze artists, jugglers, even high wire acts, became part of a film and music hall mix.

William Taylor himself, with his imperial beard, top hat and frock coat was to be lost to the fairground when shows went off the road at the outbreak of the First World War. However, he had forseen this eventuality and his 'New Electric Palace' at Calne was waiting as a cinema to host the moving pictures that had served the travelling showmen so well.

54. A unique photograph taken from a glass plate of the bioscope scene at Bulwell Wakes, Nottingham in 1903. ***(Author)***

55. The scene at those same Wakes but opposite the Bioscopes. ***(Author)***

56. Posing for the camera on Twigdon's Coliseum. ***(Rutland Cottage Music and Fairground museum)***

57. The fairground scene in front of Taylor's 'Wardculargraph', said to be the 'acme of living pictures'. *(Author)*

58. The frontage of Aspland's Bioscope show. *(Author)*

59. It was admission 2d with children charged 1d as these performers enticed fairgoers to watch the Aspland performance. *(Peter Trueman)*

60. 'You must laugh, you Cannot help it' said the banner as a girl entertainer poses on the steps to Aspland's show. *(Peter Trueman)*

61. Jacob Studt's 2nd Bioscope show in Orton and Spooners Yard about 1907.
(Rutland Cottage Music and Fairground Museum)

62. The show front that brought in the crowds with some of the entertainers who provided the 'free' outside show. *(Author)*

63. **William Taylor's Bioscope with William Taylor at the front encouraging the crowds forward.** ***(Author)***

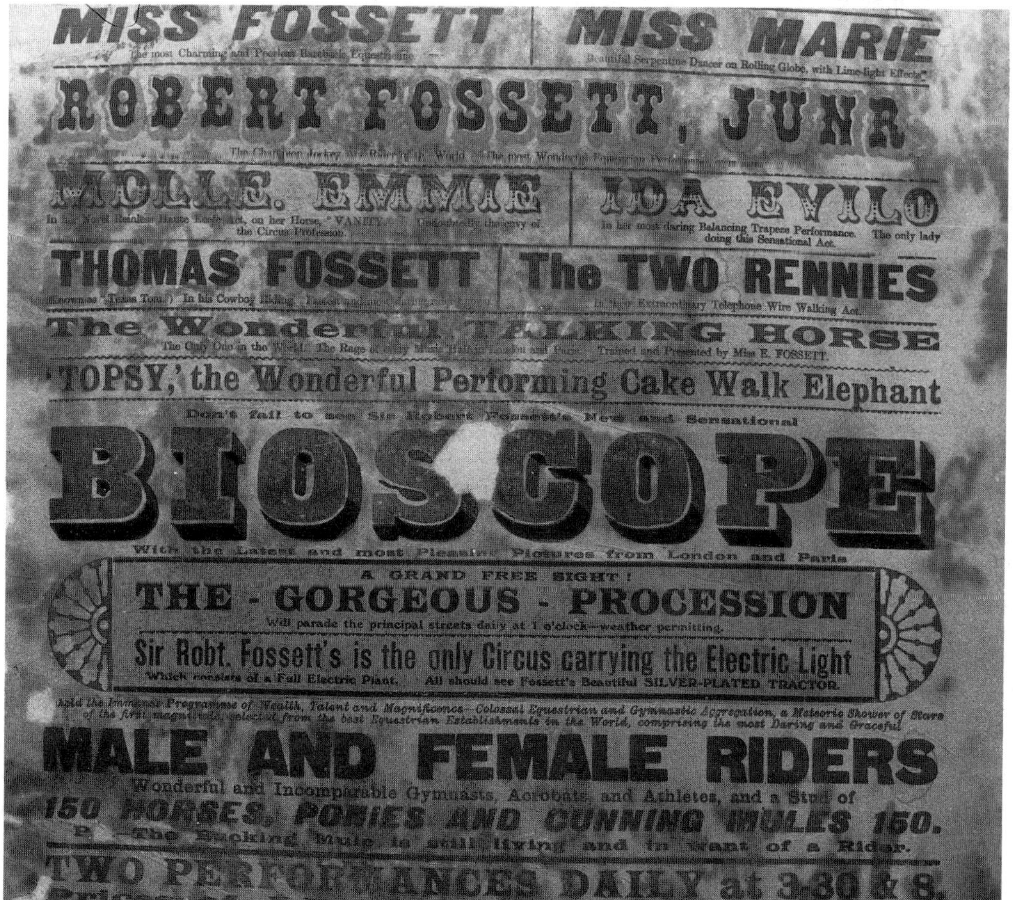

64. **Bioscopes became part and parcel of the touring circus as this old poster shows.** ***(Rutland Cottage Music and Fairground Museum)***

CHAPTER SEVEN

THE RIDES

No one knows for certain when rides found their way onto the fair. Early roundabouts were primitive affairs and designed to entertain the children. Of necessity they were of simple construction, consisting of little else than a circular platform suspended by rods from a centre pole with a series of seats on the platform for their young riders. In England the roundabout received its first mention during the eighteenth century, with Steven's immortal phrase, 'Here's the Merry-go-rounds, come who rides, come who rides, Sir' in his poem describing St Bartholomew's Fair in August, 1729.

The earliest photographic evidence of a riding machine dates from about 1860 and depicts Twigdon's Riding Machine, believed to be at Dunton Bassett, Leicestershire. This was a circular platform suspended by rods from a central pole with a number of horses mounted on the platform. Although it again was obviously designed for children, it appeared suitable for adults as well.

The reason for the introduction of wooden horses to act as seats is also unclear. 'Lord' George Sanger recalled how a home-made roundabout of this type, built by his father about 1836, was propelled by boys who, '......having no half pennies of their own, were always prepared to push their luckier companions for the reward of a ride later on'. Sanger described the ride in his book, 'Seventy Years A Showman' and gives the following description of the primitive roundabout. '....The horses were enlarged examples of the rough penny toys. Their legs were simply stiff round sticks, their bodies were lumps of deal, rounded on one side, their heads were roughly cut from half inch deal boards and roughly inserted in a groove in their bodies, while the tails and manes were made of strips of rabbit skin. They were gaudy animals, being white plentiful dotted with red and blue spots.' It could be that some of these early 'roundabouts' were even the work of a local wheelwright as there are descriptions of 'great cart wheels' which had seats fastened to their circumferences.

The centre pole on which the wheel revolved was as important as the wheel itself. As the roundabout evolved, this centre pole was enlarged and supported in a hole cut through two large pieces of timber formed into a cross. Four stays ran to form the cross section to support the centre pole in an upright position. Now the wheel could be positioned higher up that centre pole and the carriages for the riders could be suspended from the spokes that were fitted into the central hub.

Swings in their basic form were another obvious attraction at early fairs. In the beginning they would have possibly carried but one rider. Progression then saw the basic design advance so that several passengers could ride at the same time. These basically consisted of two end 'A' frames and a cross bar from which swung a large boat which gained momentum through men pulling down on ropes at one end of the ride.

By the 1800s the forerunner of the Big Wheel, the over-boats had arrived. Highly ornate boats were suspended within two parallel square frames which were connected through the centre by an axle. A passenger carrying car was suspended, swinging freely, from each corner and frame and cars were supported by two sets of legs, allowing the frame to rotate. When they arrived on the fair they were cranked by the only means available, muscle power.

Gravity slides must have been known from early times, but it was not until the early nineteen hundreds that the first Helter Skelter towers, sometimes called the Lighthouse Slip, often shortened to Slip, were opened by Jacob Studt, T. Harrison of Preston and Relph & Pedley.

These had the advantage that there were no working parts, the riders sliding down the spiral pathway by gravity.

The early slips were often a little difficult to build up and there were problems in very windy weather. However, once erected they were solid and trouble free. They were, and indeed still are, the beacons that carry the fairground message over long distances at night and even the early example illustrated has a light towards the top.

Numerically, the early riding machines were of little relative importance, for the fair was still shows and exhibitions. Here would be found the boxers and wrestlers, the juggling groups and acrobats, the dioramas, peep shows and freaks as well as games of skill and performing animals. Country fairs could be centred round nothing more than a couple of swings or a single early wooden roundabout, and everything had to be moved to and fro by horses for, without a suitable form of motive power, it was impossible for the riding machines to develop to any great degree.

There was progress in the size of the roundabout. The number of radiating spokes gradually increased so that there could be up to eight pairs of horses and two carriages suspended from the 'wheel'. The carriages were of particular importance to the ride owner. Carrying up to six people, they were ideally suited to the use of ladies who could now 'ride the roundabout' with their men folk. The horses were suspended by rods passing through the body so that the riders could sit abreast, feet in stirrups as a real horseman would do. All this added to the weight of the ride, and in place of boys, a pony was harnessed to the inner side of one of the carriages, wearing a brightly coloured harness fitted with bells. When the showman rang his own bell to signal the start of the ride, the pony began its twelve revolutions and then stopped for another load of passengers.

While the lack of motive power held back the development of the early amusements at the fair, and prior to the 1870s the roundabouts that existed were restricted in their capacity to carry paying passengers, hand cranked street roundabouts were a common sight in Victorian cities.

Henry Thurston, the founder of the famous Eastern Counties section family of that name began his fairground career with just such a ride. This was a horse drawn four wheeled flat cart with the hand operated children's roundabout on top of it. He travelled the district whenever he could charging one half penny per ride. So successful was it, and so many were the demands for his attendance at events of all types, that what began as a part time venture saw him finish his work in a local brickyard and take on the role of a travelling showman. To eliminate the costly manual labour needed to operate the machine, he had it converted to pony power. Not only this, but he experimented with ideas to bring an up and down or 'galloping' motion to the horses. He took his basic findings to two friends, William Reynolds and Charles King and there is a patent dated 1885 by Reynolds and King for what is generally accepted as the first 'overhead' crank action system for a galloping horse roundabout.

Then, to the delight of those who could only gaze in envy at those wealthy enough to enjoy the delights of the 'velocipede' or cycle, the 1860s saw Frederick Savage, the King's Lynn ride builder, introduce a 'velocipide' ride. This consisted of a single row of eighteen wheels running round a grooved track. It was ideal for the showman as the riders provided the propulsion and even paid for the privilege.

Although the 'machines' were attached to each other, a free wheel device compensated for varying strengths among the riders. There was also a braking system whereby the operator could control the length of the ride, although this could present difficulties. There were many instances when the combined forces of riders determined to prolong their 'bicycling' experiences defeated every attempt to bring them to a stop. On one infamous occasion it was only when fatigue overtook the riders that the owner could claim his machine back!

The fairground was now, however, approaching the age of steam. Free from the restrictions of man or horse power, a new breed of ride manufacturers, headed by the 'Father of them all', Frederick Savage of King's Lynn, was going to create an age of glory that many believe has never been equalled in the later history of the Mart.

65. Twigdon's Riding Machine built circa 1855. Believed photographed at Dunton Bassett, Leicestershire about 1860. *(Loughborough Markets and Fairs Department)*

66. A primitive roundabout used in the Middle East about 1914. *(Author)*

67. Arab children enjoying a ride in a home-made swing boat. Photograph taken at the same time. *(Author)*

68. Buckland Bros Dobby set as presented at the 1975 King's Lynn Festival. The roundabout, believed then to be over one hundred years old was originally operated by a 'bell' pony. When the showman's bell indicated the start of each ride, the pony began to trot round for the twelve revolutions that was the duration. *(Author)*

Previous page
69. Old time overboats also at the Lynn Festival. *(Author)*

70. A family group posing on the front of Spencer's Mystic Joy Wheel. Date and location unknown. *(Roger Tuby)*

71. The 'Racers' at Loughborough Mart, circa 1894. *(Loughborough Markets and Fairs Department)*

This page
72. Hand powered roundabouts. These machines consisted of centre pole, cheese, cradle ring, gearwork, spars and quarterings, twenty four horses, with bridles and stirrups, horses rods, top, bottom and middle centres, painted, stencilled and varnished. *(Savage Catalogue, 1902)*

73. A set of Savage Tandem Bicycles. The ride consisted of twelve tandem bicycles with solid rubber tyres and electro-plated handlebars. *(Savage Catalogue, 1902)*

74. Llanelly Pleasure Fair, showing Savage built Amusements, Shows and Rides including overboats and a shooter at the bottom left. *(Rutland Cottage Music and Fairground Museum)*

CHAPTER EIGHT

THE ARRIVAL OF STEAM

Although he was hardly likely to have appreciated it at the time, Sydney George Soames, another of that forward looking race of village engineers, started what can only be described as a fairground revolution when, in the village of Marsham some ten miles from Norwich, in the mid 1860s, he harnessed steam to drive a roundabout at North Aylsham fair. True, he was possibly not the first, there had been references to an earlier steam driven ride in Yorkshire. However, it was Soames who is credited with that initial breakthrough that brought steam to the fairground. He appears to have been a modest man for the subsequent development of steam powered amusements was left to others. But from that humble beginning using, it is believed, a portable engine, came the great ride manufacturers of the steam age. The most celebrated were Frederick Savage of King's Lynn, Tidman and Sons of Norwich and Thomas Walker of Tewkesbury.

As well as bringing about a new era in fairground amusements, steam brought a decline in some of our smaller fairs. Village fairs were modest gatherings in the days that George Soames turned his attention to fairground motive power. Their emphasis was firmly on attractions such as wrestlers, jugglers, peep shows, freaks and exhibitions. There were the usual games of skill and strength and what roundabouts or swingboats were there, worked either by human or pony power, were numerically of little importance. The arrival of steam altered completely the balance of the fair. The new steam driven roundabouts were the rage for the public, pushing the age old shows into the background.

And as they involved considerable financial outlay on the part of their owners, often on hire purchase terms, large crowds had to be almost guaranteed before these new riding masters would attend a fair. This meant that they needed the larger fairs and as the steam age progressed some of the smaller villages completely lost their traditional fairs as the other entertainers also congregated where the crowds were assured. This state of affairs, however, would hardly have been recognised when people like Frederick Savage began to take the first steps in harnessing steam to mechanical rides.

It is said that his first steam engine came after a visit to King's Lynn fair where he told a man laboriously cranking an organ that he would make him a small steam engine to do the task. The result was a single cylinder engine with governors and pump, mounted on a locomotive type boiler and contained on a truck fitted with castors. A number of showland personalities are believed to have responded, including Randall Williams.

Frederick Savage was indeed to emerge from the steam era as the 'Father of the Fairground'. For his innovative mind was to provide the showmen with rides that were breathtaking to a fairgoing public that up to then had had to be content with what muscle and pony power could provide.

Small semi-portable engines were also being taken into use on shooting galleries, with a two-fold purpose, either pumping the water jets that held the target ping pong balls, or driving a slowly moving belt containing the ducks that were the target. During the two years that followed the steam driven Velocipede, Frederick Savage converted a 'dobby' roundabout owned by William Sanger to steam drive. This was followed by other successful conversions, both of 'dobby' sets and manually propelled Velocipedes.

Steam evolved dramatically when Frederick Savage introduced his 'centre engine'. This became the heart of all round rides, with the exception of the Steam Velocipedes, which Frederick Savage patented with Pat Collins. It consisted of a sprung centre truck, incorporating the actual engine itself, the gearing and drive shaft, in fact everything for the roundabout to be built up from it. With polished brass fittings, gun metal gauges, twisted governor column and steam whistles to get the crowds round, they were typical examples of the engineering skills that brought the Savage works universal acclaim.

On roundabouts, up to the mid 1880s, the horses were hung on pivots and there was no platform fitted. Although this gave a form of swinging action to the riders, there was no control on the pivots and horses swinging outwards as the ride speed increased. Then, following an idea put forward by the East Anglia showman, Henry Thurston, the Cambridgeshire firm of Reynolds and King developed a double overhead crank action that, although there was still no platform, prevented unwanted fore and aft swinging yet allowing some swinging out by centrifugal force as the ride revolved. The patent, which was granted in 1885, also brought leg movements through a lever system inside the bodies of the horse. It was complex, however, and would obviously suffer under the stresses of building up, pulling down and then building up yet again.

Tidman's were next on the scene with a platform added to another single crank horse movement. However, it was Savage, through a patent finalised in 1893, which brought the 'galloper' action as it is recognised today. This 'bounding' movement, similar to the action of galloping horses, was brought about by overhead cranks to which horse rods were attached. Then came a bottom platform with steps for the use of passengers mounting the ride. To ensure the safety of the riders when the machines were revolving at speed, the horse rods were extended to pass through the the bottom platform. Slotted holes were fitted in the platform to allow some 10 to 15 degrees swing as the speed of the ride increased.

Now they were providing centre engines, manufacturers could increase the size of the spinning frame and less than three decades after Soames's initial experiments, three and four abreast sets were being built with diameters between 36 and 48 feet.

The switchback was a ride that would have been impossible without steam. Here the punters enjoyed the delights of a series of eight coupled cars which travelled round a circular track running over two hills and hollows. Frederick Savage had the advantage over other manufacturers that he was now clear to develop the undulating track the ride needed and on which there would be no danger of derailment. In the past there had been a tendency for the front wheels of the cars to leave the track as they reached the summit of each hill.

Savage's solution was to add a third rail which contained only the front wheels of each car and to elongate the summits so they were almost in line with the car's wheelbase, giving a more oval than round shape to the track. Once the mechanics had been perfected, the ride developed rapidly. The centre pole became the centre chimney for the engine and in the switchback, this was extended and a covering top made. The visual appearance was dramatically increased with the addition of rounding boards, droppers and domes. Such was the search for perfection that the actual carving and decoration became a skill in its own right and firms came into being that specialised in this side of ride manufacture. Of these possibly the best known was Orton, Sons and Spooner of

Burton on Trent.

Organs began to appear in front of the centre engine, those humble cars that were fitted to the first switchbacks were replaced by superb venetian gondolas whose carving and decoration matched the rest of the ride and by installing eccentrics a rolling and pitching motion could enhance the feeling of those Venetian Gondolas on their canals.

Ever ready to give their public a taste of the latest in mechanical innovations, when motor cars appeared on the roads showmen ensured that imitation but totally realistic cars took over from the Venetian gondola and also the roundabout horses.

Platform rides, however, were far from dead. Frederick Savage in conjunction with 'Lord' George Sanger produced a Steam 'Sea on Land' ride with about twenty sets being constructed between 1880 and 1885. The punters rode in yachts and a gearing underneath brought a pitching and rocking motion that to the public of the age was as realistic as going to sea. The ride, however, was to bring tragedy into Frederick Savage's life. For while his son-in-law was demonstrating the 'Sea on Land' his wife fell onto the tramway and suffered such serious injuries that it was necessary to amputate both legs.

Proving that there is nothing ever really new, a proposal for a tunnel under the English Channel from England to France brought yet another novelty ride, the 'Tunnel Railway'. A track 40ft in diameter was laid for a 2ft gauge steam locomotive and carriages that circled it, running half in the outside light and half in a darkened tunnel. One famous showman to operate the ride was George Thomas Tuby, renowned for his civic duties as well as his life as a showman. However he was to remark that it was never popular with English riders although it went very well when he sold it in France. His own views were that for courting couples the tunnel was neither long enough nor dark enough!

In the late 1880s the Tilt-o-Whirl or Razzle Dazzle made an appearance. Essentially this was a flat round platform, fitted with seats and an outer wall. It was pivoted on its central pole so that it tilted as it revolved.

Steam was also harnessed to what became one of the most popular rides on the fairground, the Steam Yachts. These were a development of a steam swing which was introduced in the late 1880s by William Cartwright and Henry Cracknell. But it was when Frederick Savage turned his attentions to the rides that they became known as the Steam Yachts. The drive came from a central portable steam engine which was connected by a chain to the twin pair of boats, each capable of carrying up to thirty paying passengers. Even today one set, the yachts that Harry Lee made famous, have survived and still prove themselves an irresistible attraction to young and old alike.

The development of the fairground rides brought about a marked a change in emphasis. In the early days, the primitive rides of the age were intended as attractions for children. Elders, if they paid attention at all, were merely onlookers to what many must have seen as intruders among the established traditional fairground pleasures. That changed with the pre-steam arrival of the Velocipede rides and the progression of the roundabout into an adult as well as juvenile ride. Steam undoubtedly enriched the fairground with a previously unimagined variety but it was to show that, through the traction engines that served the fairground up to the Second World War, this was yet another beginning.

75. Savage Switchback Roundabout. The ride consisted of a set of eight cars running over an undulating railway. A 4 hp double cylinder engine, mounted on a specially designed truck with all driving gears, accessories and the necessary tools was provided. All rods were covered with twisted brass. ***(Savage Catalogue, 1902)***

76. **Anderton and Rowlands Scenic Motor cars.** ***(Author)***

77. **Walter Holland's Steam Yachts. Date and venue unknown. In their heyday in the 1920s a set of Steam Yachts could be bought for about £1,500 and at some of the larger fairs it was not uncommon to find five sets at one fair.** ***(Author)***

78. Old Mr Redfern Snr photographed with some of his staff. As motor cars advanced in popularity cars replaced horses etc on fairground rides as this undated photograph, believed at a Yorkshire fair, shows.
(Rennie Crick)

79. Again although the date and venue are unknown, this photograph as the Ayres family pose for the camera is symbolic of the fairground's age of achievement.
(Author)

80. An unusual ride was Reuben Holdsworth's Flying Pigs and Waltzing Balloons with pigs and balloons in place of the other animals. At the time balloons were a definite innovation because they revolved on their own axes as the ride went round. An unusual feature was that the top roundings went clockwise while the ride itself travelled anti clockwise, giving a greater impression of speed.
(Rutland Cottage Music and Fairground Museum)

THE
ELITE
MELLOR'S

Previous page
81. Mellor's three abreast gallopers built by Walkers' of Tewkesbury in 1924. The photograph was taken at Holmewood near Chesterfield in the 1930s. Words on rounding boards, 'Mellors Grand Electric Easy Riding. Patronized by the Elite'. Also in photograph are Jim Bishton's Hoopla and Dobbies. *(Ray Maddison)*

82. Hibble and Mellors Gallopers this time provide a background for an interesting photograph of children, possibly from the Nazareth Orphanage, Nottingham. *(Ray Maddison)*

83. A family photograph on Harniess Bros 1892 Savage Three A Breast, mixed horses, cockerels and ostriches. Later it was fitted with all cockerels. Sold to William Church. *(Roger Tuby)*

84. Another ride in the Harniess family was their Flying Horses that later went to Sam Crow and then Danny Hammer. *(Roger Tuby)*

85. It was a true 'age of achievement' for the Twigdon family who progressed from that early primitive roundabout to rides that included the Sea on Land. ***(Nottingham Markets and Fairs Department)***

86. An undated photograph of Jacob Studt's three abreast. ***(Author)***

87. Ulverston White Fair, 1924 showing Emmerson's Jumpers and Taylor Bros Steam Switch Back Motors. *(Author)*

CHAPTER NINE

SHOWMEN'S ENGINES

Steam, of course, brought another advantage for the showmen. It released them from the limitations of horse power in moving their amusements from fair to fair. With a showman's road locomotive, not only could the size and weight of the loads be increased, the time on the road was reduced. The transfer from horses to steam, however, was more than merely investing in a road locomotive, often financed on credit terms, adding to the hire purchase commitments already involved in the steam ride. Few of the travelling showmen had any direct experience of steam and they had to rely on outsiders recruited to drive the engine.

The nature of the business, the long hours, the seasonable work, the rough living standards, mostly meant that these engine drivers were hardly the pick of the profession. More important they may not have been used to the long wagon trains involved, particularly during adverse weather conditions. As a result there were a number of accidents caused when the drivers, through inexperience of showland driving, tried the impossible when it came to getting that wagon train up or down steep slopes without uncoupling some of them.

Showmen had always been quick learners and it was not long before they knew more about their engines than this first imported breed of driver. This led to a better class of man joining the fairground steam age, and many stayed in the business until the decline of the road locomotive in fairground service.

However, it was not only drivers who caused problems for these early steam pioneers. While they were faster than horses, travel was still slow. The 'Red Flag' regulations meant that even showmen had to have a man with a red flag walking in front of the engine. Speed limits were imposed so that officially traction engines could not exceed four miles per hour on the open road and two miles per hour in built up areas. Arthur Stanford, in an issue of the Fairground Society's 'Jottings', recalls a case in Derbyshire where two engines were racing side by side, travelling all of ten miles per hour, according to police evidence, with the red flag men on the roofs of the engines insulting each other! The crews are said to have been fined 2/6d by the magistrates.

The actual wagons had to be altered and adapted. For whereas, when horses were the motive power, up to eight trucks would be needed to move a set of gallopers from fair to fair, the steam engine reduced that to half, itself drawing the centre truck, horse truck, organ truck and platform truck. Horses travelled slower than the road locomotives and it had been necessary to stop often to rest and feed them. Now, with higher speeds and longer distances between breaks, it was soon discovered that wooden hubs and iron or steel axles were hardly the ideal companions. Overheating and the consequent risk of fire was a constant threat in those early days. Ingenuity has always been an integral part of life for the showman and it was not long before cast iron bushes were being fitted into the wooden hubs. This, however, was not the perfect solution. There was still a danger that the bush would work loose. The friction from the bush rotating about the hub brought back the heat problem and the fire risk. Because of this, until the wagons came to be fitted with an improved wheel and hub, staff could be seen running alongside the road train, anxiously looking for those tell tale puffs of blue smoke.

While the ride owners could possibly afford and justify a new road locomotive, those with smaller attractions were once again on the outside looking in. Not only were they unable to afford this luxury until that first generation of steam engines was replaced by the ride owners, and their previous engines came on the market second-hand, though even a seven horsepower engine might have been too large for their requirements. This class of showmen then looked for a second-hand steam tractor or even a steam wagon. However, there were cases where the smaller amusement proprietors ignored the steam engine period, remaining faithful to their horses until the First World War when they made the change direct from horses to the internal combustion engine.

The size of the wagon trains became legend. William Murphy, writing to John Fowler & Co in November, 1895, recalled an occasion in Jarrow-on-Tyne when he had ten wagons behind the engine and the train was in three streets at the same time. Even in winter he said he could cover thirty miles in a day with the engine working in front of a load weighing fifty tons. This could have related to 'The Belle of the Road', a Class B4. double crank compound supplied by Fowlers in August of that year.

When it came to moving the long wagon trains on the public roads there was consideration for other road users. To this end some used a spring loaded hammer bell inside the cab. A length of cord was attached to it and this ran the length of the wagons being pulled. This gave the workers on the wagons a means of communication with the driver who, in towns and villages, could be out of sight of some of the wagons.

A single pull on the rope and the sounding of the bell on the footplate was the signal to stop. Two rings and the driver knew that he had to move on. If traffic began to queue behind the wagons, the crew would give three pulls and the driver pulled to the side of the road in a position where the following traffic could overtake safely. In turn the driver used his steam whistle to communicate with those on the wagons. A single blast told them to apply the brakes and a double blast was the signal to release them.

Permits were part and parcel of the daily life for those who used these heavy engines on the road after the coming of the internal combustion engine. One was needed from each local authority through whose area the engine was to pass. If they were to go through five counties on the way from one fair to another five permits would be needed. The permits were for a period specified on them and usually application was made by post some days in advance of the journey. However, there were occasions when a last minute decision was taken as to the fair attended. There could be a word of mouth recommendation for a particular fair that made that individual decide on a change of location or he could hear of one needing just the attraction he had. Then a new set of travel permits had to be obtained. If their areas of travel were covered by the railway system, these presented few problems. In other cases a permit would be obtained for the nearest county and then couriers sent ahead to get the other permits and meet the road train as it approached that county boundary. Usually the permit would have the condition that the showman was responsible for paying for any damage caused to the road surface, bridges etc. These conditions were taken very seriously and it was not unknown for them to put down grit so that no damage was caused to a tarmac surface on a hot afternoon.

Then in the 1920s it became unlawful to use an engine on a road unless it was fitted with rubber tyres. This caused some showmen considerable expense. However, their ingenuity came to the fore as George Rhodes Tuby recalls.

He can remember how a fortnight was spent at Bently Fair fitting rubber tyres to the Burrell, 'Norah'. Second-hand solid tyres were bought from Doncaster Corporation Transport and these ex-bus tyres were cut and fitted to the engine with the wheels being drilled with a ratchet drill, hard work indeed for young George.

Then it was the turn of the railway companies to fight back for the freight they were losing to road transport. One method was to impose weight restrictions on steam engines using their road bridges over railway lines. We then had the situation that while a steam road train could not cross, the same load could be pulled over with a team of horses!

The hardships associated with fairground steam travel were vividly illustrated by the late Jack Collins in *A Showman's Life*. He was born in 1880 and at an early age, through the teachings of his father, was thoroughly conversant with their showman's engine. By the time he was in his early teens, when generators had been fitted, he was in charge of an engine providing power for the steam roundabout lights. Early electric lighting was a novelty to the fair goers and nothing delighted young Jack Collins more than mystifying the punters by flashing the blades of his penknife across the dynamo, creating a magnet to pick up small pieces of metal.

In this age of 'first come, first served', on the fairground, Jack Collins, in later life, would think nothing of securing his men on one of the wagons after pull down, so they could sleep, and drive and steer the engine with its wagon load and living van through the night so they got a prime position at the new venue. Often the footplate got so hot that the only way to get his shoes off swollen feet was to slit them open.

There was, of course, always a need for coal and water. Adequate amounts would be taken on before leaving the fairground. If there was a danger of the coal running low then someone would be sent on ahead on the cycle almost all showmen carried, to arrange for the necessary supplies. Water could present far more serious problems, particularly during night travel when it was easy to miss streams and ponds. If their water got too low, the lead core plug in the firebox would melt when the boiler became empty. Now there would be no alternative but to rake out the fire and wait until it was cool enough to remove the ashes and firebars. The driver then had the distinctly unpopular job of crawling underneath the engine, and up into the firebox to fit a replacement plug.

While the driver was possibly cursing his luck at the engine, the men were out in the dark in their search for water that would be brought to the engine by the water dandy which was a permanent addition on the back of most waggon trains. Then the fire had to be laid and started and it was a case of waiting until the pressure was high enough for the journey to continue. Most drivers tried to be particularly careful that this fate was for others rather than them. And in the views of many, the drivers of the showland engines became an elite, the cream of the steam age drivers. Unlike their counterparts in village and town, during the travelling season from February to November, they had no base to return to for repairs.

During this time it was essential that the engine was available for work both on the fairground itself and for haulage. These showland drivers developed such a pride in their work that their engines were always in tip top condition. And when it came to repairs they proved capable of tackling almost any job that came along. Traction engines on the fair would be given daily maintenance. There was the oiling to be done, the firebox cleaning out before another fire was lit and the brasses and other metal parts to be cleaned until they were gleaming. For to most ride owners, their engines were a vital part of their show, and if they were proud of their attractions, they were equally proud of the engines and this was reflected in their appearance. And, to ensure that everything was kept in first class order, the boiler was drained and washed out after one hundred hours of service to remove any rust and silt.

There was another difference between fairground steam and that used in agriculture or road haulage. For while the load behind these engines could be nothing more valuable than farm produce or road making materials, the showman's wagon train could consist of their entire fairground equipment valued at thousands of pounds. In these circumstances it was hardly surprising that the showman himself or his son took responsibility for driving the engine with the womanfolk often taking over the steering.

Accidents with these huge engines were rare. When they did occur it was usually a case of a surface giving way because of the weight of the engine and its loads. However, there were occasions when the engine with its load behind got out of control and with spectacular results. One of the most remarkable of these was in June, 1908 when the engine, the Burrell 'Reliance' No 2979, owned by Relph and Pedley, together with the living van and two other trailers left the road and plunged into the lake at Thirlmere, unfortunately killing the driver. The engine, then only three months old, was submerged in the lake. However, it was salvaged and sent in pieces back to the Burrell works at Thetford where it was re-built to emerge as No 3038, 'The Prince' to work with Reuben Holdsworth's 'Flying Pigs and Waltzing Balloons'.

It is virtually impossible to give the exact number of engines in showland use because many were normal road locomotives converted for showmen. However, possibly more than 1,000 engines of various types served the fairground community in the steam era.

The most prolific builders were Burrell, closely followed by Fowler. Both made in excess of 300 'showmans locomotives', more than twice the number of their nearest rival, Fosters.

The first locomotive made by Burrell for showland service was No 1287, an 8 hp single cylinder, completed in June, 1887 for William Shipley of Driffield, Yorkshire while Fowler produced their Class A Double Crank Compound No 4765 for Reynolds and King in May of the previous year.

Other builders were Aveling & Porter, Foden, Garrett, Ruston & Hornsby who made the 6 hp compound 'Emperor' for Henry Thurston in March, 1887, McLaren, Ransome, Savage and Wallis & Steevens. Savage also built traction centres, an attempt to use the same engine for haulage and driving the ride, although these were never popular with showmen.

Nearly every driver of the age would claim that his engine was the best, no matter what make it was. In reality, however, it would appear that while the Burrell would speed along with its load in flat countryside, when it came to hills Fowlers reigned supreme, with Fosters a close second.

The early engines were seen by their owners as prime movers of the new breed of steam rides. However, the wonder of the age for Victorians in the 1870s and 80s was electric lighting, and it was not long before the showmans engine was generating electricity, first for illumination on rides and then to power another new breed of ride.

88. A showman's group round an early motor lorry with the living van in tow. Driving is Tommy Angelo who married Alice Crick, (Right to left) Owner Henry Redfern, Tommy Crick, Benny Mitchell, Lancashire showman, 'Sammy' who worked for Henry Crick. *(Rennie Crick)*

89. A Savage Traction Centre Engine. *(Savage Catalogue, 1902)*

90. An undated photograph of T. Harniess' Fowler, 'Jubilee', with their Grand Roundabout and living vans. ***(Rennie Crick)***

91,92 & 93. Serious accidents were rare in the age of steam. One exception was in June, 1908, when a road train, traction engine, living van and two trailers left the road at Thirlmere and plunged into the lake killing the driver. The Burrell 2979 Reliance was completely submerged. The engine belonging to Relph and Pedley was a mere three months old. It was recovered and sent in pieces to the builders. It was rebuilt and repaired and emerged as 3038, 'The Prince' for Reuben Holdsworth's Flying Porkers. ***(Rutland Cottage Music and Fairground Museum)***

93.

94,95 & 96. Here the 1908 Fowler, No 11419, 'General White' first sold to H. Steel Parry, also of Cardiff, before being sold to White Bros of Cardiff performs a sad duty as it waits to move away the late John White. In the centre is his son, Sidney White who arranged for the funeral cortege to be headed by the suitably decorated engine. The popularity and respect the family held in the city is shown through the crowds that flocked the route.
(Peter Trueman)

Top right, page 61

97. A mystery picture. The engine is undoubtedly the 1912 Wallis and Steevens 7 nhp compound No 7192 bought by Mrs Amy Lock of Plymouth in 1915 and converted into a showman's engine. In 1937 it was named 'Queen Elizabeth'. But what is the miniature engine doing in the photograph and what was the purpose of the reflectors? *(Author)*

98. 'Lord James' was a Fowler B.6. compound engine, No 11846, built in 1909. It was sold to J & R.M. Williams Co. Durham and named after Randell Monte Williams' second son. ***(Author)***

99. Hibble and Mellor's Foster, 'Success' in 1939. The 65 bhp engine No 14632 was built in February, 1934 and sold to Mr Carl Mumby of Cleethorpes in 1940. In 1956 it was saved from the scrap yard and it came into preservation. *(Ray Maddison)*

100. Another Foster that saw service with Hibble and Mellor was No 14627, 'Progress' built on the 14th September, 1931, seen here with David Limb. *(Ray Maddison)*

CHAPTER TEN

ELECTRICITY ARRIVES FOR FAIRGROUND OWNERS

The dazzling and brilliant light which could be obtained by transmitting a powerful electric current between two sticks of carbon was first shown to the Royal Institute by Sir Humphrey Davey in 1813. This, of necessity, had to employ a battery containing no less than 2,000 cells. An additional drawback was that as the carbon rods got smaller during their gradual consumption, there was no way of keeping the gap between them constant. However, by the early 1850s regulators were developed that solved the problem.

Electricity may have arrived, but for the showman, to whom it could have provided both lighting and power, the insurmountable obstacle was the massive batteries required. Show folk could only watch with envy as this new form of lighting appeared in halls and houses. Then came the breakthrough they had been waiting for. With Faraday's discovery of magnetic electric induction, the dynamo and generator became a practical proposition. The first generating plant capable of being mounted on a traction engine was the work of R. E. B. Crompton who, in 1879, designed just such equipment for Marshalls of Gainsborough. In July of that year, it is recorded, one of these Marshall-Crompton engines was used to illuminate the Henley Regatta. As can be imagined, the event drew crowds in their thousands, but not all came merely to see and marvel. Many, failing to understand these latest scientific advances and fearful for the future, made determined attempts to sabotage the engine and generators. Fortunately, Marshalls had been prepared for this eventuality, and men from Gainsborough, armed with heavy spanners, successfully fought off the intending saboteurs.

Then in 1889 Avelings exhibited at the Paris Exhibition a single cylinder road locomotive but with a platform erected over the front of the hornplates carrying a generator driven off a cast iron gear ring bolted to the flywheel spokes. Show people were not slow to realise the potential this gave of generating electricity at the fair. However, lighting as provided on the rides and shows in the early 1900s was by arc lights, with the sparking carbon rods covered by a wired glass globe. The Aveling position for the generator was soon replaced by what became the standard on this class of engines, above and in front of the smoke box. At first the generator platform was an addition fitted above the smokebox, but some builders such as Burrell made it an integral part, following the curve of the boiler and smokebox itself.

It was about 1912 that, through the advent of electricity and the generator on the showman's engines, fiction could turn almost into reality with the dummy motor cars on switchback rides being fitted with electric motors to the rear of each car and connected by chain drive to the rear axles.

It was electricity that brought the advance from the basic switchback to the scenic, one of the most impressive rides ever to be seen on the fairground. With an outside diameter of about 55 ft, a height of almost 30 ft and eight cars coupled onto a continuous train running on a circular track with a gauge about 2 ft 7 in, with two hills and valleys, they were fairgoers' delights. Visually they have never been equalled. For with the centre engine and driving frame no longer needed, there was a large area of internal space that ride manufacturers, particularly the Burton on Trent based Orton and Spooner, used to the full. The massive organs that had once been the outside centrepiece for the travelling bioscopes but which had drifted into oblivion as they were replaced by the permanent picture houses, came into their own again, becoming the centrepiece for this new breed of ride, and at the back of the organ truck could be a waterfall and appropriate hillside scenery.

There was outside carving, domes and droppers and even matching hand rails. The motor car, however, was no longer the novelty it had been in the days of the switchback and after the 1914-18 war, they gave way on the scenics to exotic dragons, whales, dolphins and peacocks, each a tribute to the carver and decorator's craft. Once again Frederick Savage was to the fore, giving the fairs their first Scenic, with the current to the live rails coming from the generator of the showman's road locomotive.

Like any other advance on the fairground, the transition from steam to electric power was not without its headaches. One of the difficulties was in getting a slow start when the scenic was loaded with paying passengers. The answer came in the form of a special scenic showman's engine, first introduced by Burrell. These were fitted with a larger boiler and there was space between the chimney and the cylinders to carry an 'exciter', a smaller dynamo driven by a belt from the main generator.

Using this system the power output from the main engine generator could be varied by increasing or reducing the current that was creating the magnetic field of the main generator by current from the exciter dynamo so that the engine was turning over at a constant speed all the time.

Some existing engines were returned to Thetford to have the platform and auxiliary dynamo fitted. In July 1912, No 3163, 'Doncaster' which had been new to G.T. Tuby of Doncaster in 1910, was returned for this purpose.

With the cars of the scenic rides weighing up to one ton, there were inevitably difficulties in both building up the ride and pulling it down. It soon became clear that help was needed in this direction and in their final forms these scenic engines were fitted with a crane as well as the exciter.

Impressive as the scenics were on the fairground, they were formidable machines to operate. Normally the machine and possibly the accompanying scenic engine would be bought on hire purchase. Repayments would have been high and unless the owner had a run of good fairs, he could soon be in financial trouble, for the manufacturers needed paying even at times of poor takings. At least one owner was heard to reflect that he would have been wealthier if he had never owned his scenic.

Lighter machines, however, were on their way. The 1916 Goose Fair saw its first Cake Walk and the Dodgem track was patented in 1921. They were followed by rides such as the Noah's Ark which had flexible arms fitted with a rubber tyred wheel running in a single track under the platform which carried animals or dummy motor cycles.

It was another step in this age of achievement. The thirties saw Charles Openshaw of Reading patenting the Moonrocket. Here was another new age on the Mart. The Wall of Death, the Swirl and Caterpillar, Arks and Razzle Dazzle, all contributed to the new breed of machines that followed the advent of electricity.

Collectively there is no better way to illustrate fairground evolution than to look at that last Goose Fair before the outbreak of the Second World War. Whereas in 1899 the scene in the Great Market Place was dominated by the Menageries, Bioscopes, Exhibitions and Marionettes with the 'Age of Steam' offering Roundabouts, Gondolas and Collins' Pneumatic Cycles, the scene in 1938 showed how fairground amusements had become both a profession and an industry.

From the Nottingham Markets and Fairs Department Records we know that, brought together for the last time before war was to bring a temporary end to the travelling fairs, were the Razzle Dazzle, Ark, Cake Walk and Ben Hur, Airways and Moon Rocket, the Octopus and Dodgems, Noah's Ark and Swirl, Ski Ride and Fun House, the Octopus, Big Wheel, Waltzer and Ghost Train.

However, there were still reminders of the past, like the Scenic, Yachts and Three-abreasts, and Road locomotives were still the main work-horses of the fair — but evidence for the future was to be seen.

Since the First World War, the internal combustion engine had made inroads on the Mart. Some showmen took advantage of the War Department vehicles that were for sale after the fighting finished. Many had been reconditioned before being put up for sale and offered first class service for fairground work. Many showmen, for obvious reasons, bought FWD vehicles. For while FWD was the maker's name, the letters stood for four wheel drive, and many fairs were the ideal place for the extra adhesion the chain driven wheels gave.

Other favourites were AECs and Tilling-Stevens petrol electric trucks. Here a petrol engine drove the dynamo which powered the electric motor giving the final drive. Trailer car caravans also made an appearance in the years following the end of the war.

Fairgrounds remained, however, the last bastion of the steam engine, renowned among ride owners for their reliability. When, with a view to the future, John Fowler built a diesel engined road locomotive in 1935 for the Nottingham based firm of Hibble and Mellor, with its rear 'Showman's traction engine' wheels, its ancestry was obvious though, 'Jubilee', named after that famous royal event of 1935, turned out to be a 'one off'. For whereas second-hand steam road locomotives could be obtained fairly cheaply, it was a different story with a new diesel.

The same progression was there for many individual families. True, some failed to rise above the small round and side show, but others found that fairgrounds offered them the chance of riches and social status. Who, amazed at that first humble roundabout presented by the Twigdon family in the late 1850s, could have believed that it would be the forerunner of attractions such as their Coliseum, Steam Yachts, Sea on Land or Switchback?

Here indeed were stories of progression that brought the great families into being. From small acorns mighty oaks are said to grow. What smaller beginnings could the Collins and Thurston families, to mention but two, have had, yet their growth into mighty dynasties equalled many of the success stories that steam brought to industry and commerce.

101. A photograph that reflects life on the Mart is this one of Jack Proctor's Dragons, taken at Matlock in 1914. The ride, together with two engines was later sold for £800 to Pullens when Jack Proctor was buying his Peacock Scenic. This ride eventually burned down near Sheffield. People identified include (middle row) Jobby Warwick leaning on upright, Albert Taylor in cap, Flash Brummy in white suit, George Burrows leaning on right upright. Jimmy Whiting at back, (bottom row) Johnny with pony, Albert Proctor, Jack Proctor, Billy Cross Driver, Alfie Johns, Lampman plus unknowns who could have been locals working for Proctors. ***(Ray Maddison)***

102. Hibble and Mellor's Speedway Ark built by Orton and Spooner, Burton on Trent. Their Fowler Jubilee can be seen on the left hand side. *(Ray Maddison)*

103. Hibble and Mellor's Fowler Diesel Showman's Road Locomotive, 'Jubilee'. *(Ray Maddison)*

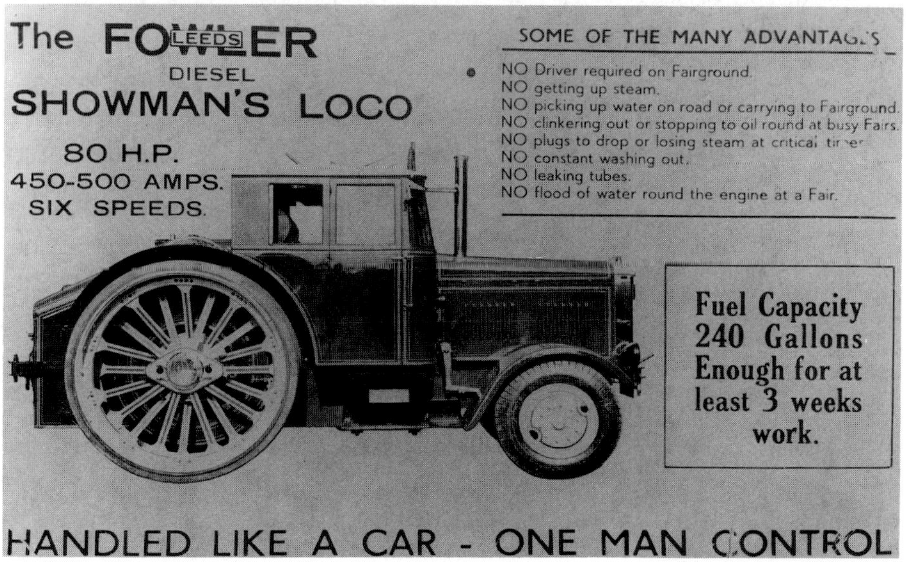

104. Fowler's advertising for the diesel showman's locomotive. *(Ray Maddison)*

105. Charles Thurston's Dragons new at King's Lynn 1920, they were later changed to Peacock cars in 1924. *(Roger Tuby)*

106. William Murphy's Scenic in North East Yorkshire, 1922. *(Roger Tuby)*

107. Cleckheaton Fair, 1907 showing Ben Howden presenting the Aspland Gondolas. *(Roger Tuby)*

108. Harniess Bros Dragon Scenic at Goole in 1932. This was formerly John Evans Motors. *(Roger Tuby)*

109. The Dive Bomber was an American invention of the late 1930s, but the rides are still attracting the customers on today's fairground. *(Author)*

110. J.P. Collins and Sons Super Waltzer at Nottingham in 1962. *(Ron Lee)*

111. The Moon Rocket and Airways were an essential part of the fairground from the 1930s.
(Nottingham Markets and Fairs Department)

112. Hibble and Mellors Monte Blanc at a Leicester Fair.
(Ray Maddison)

113-114-115-116-117-118. Morley's Golden Gallopers were a popular set of three abreasts at Nottingham Goose Fair, travelling there after the Belle View Amusement Park closed for the season.
This sequence of photographs of the build up was taken in 1962 by Ron Lee.

MORLEY'S
CHARLES
THURSTONS

MORLEY'S GRAND GOLDEN JUMPING
CHARLES
THURSTONS

ORSES ALWAYS SUPREME AND SAFE